Daily Affirmations For Women

YOUR MORNING STARTER

Wake Up To Fresh Motivation
Every Single Morning

SHERI CORTEZ

Table of Contents

Chapter 1: 20 Affirmations For Women 6

Chapter 2: 8 Ways To Gain Self-Confidence 9

Chapter 3: How To Use Affirmations For Success 13

Chapter 4: When It Is Time To Slow Down 15

Chapter 5: What Are You Measuring In Your Life? 18

Chapter 6: *Don't Live Your Life In Regret* 21

Chapter 7: Why nobody cares when you fail 24

Chapter 8: 6 Ways To Achieve Peak Performance 27

Chapter 9: 11 Ways To Attract Love 31

Chapter 10: 20 More Positive Affirmations 35

Chapter 11: Stop Wasting Time on the Details and Commit to the Fundamentals 39

Chapter 12: When It's Okay to Not Be Okay 42

Chapter 13: How To Deal With Impatience 47

Chapter 14: 6 Habits of Strong Couples 50

Chapter 15: Why Getting Started Is More Important Than Succeeding 54

Chapter 16: 10 Habits of Nancy Pelosi 57

Chapter 17: Happy People Don't Hold on To Grudges 61

Chapter 18: Happy People Have A Morning Ritual 63

Chapter 19: 5 Ways Quitting Something Can Bring You Joy ... 65

Chapter 20: 10 Habits of Kamala Harris 68

Chapter 21: 10 Stress Management Tips 72

Chapter 22: Dealing With Stress from All Angles 77

Chapter 23: How Not To Control Everything 80

Chapter 24: How To Be A Good Public Speaker 83

Chapter 25: 10 Habits of Selena Gomez 86

Chapter 26: 6 Non-violent Communication Examples For Couples ... 90

Chapter 27: Happy People Use Their Character Strengths 95
Chapter 28: 8 Ways to Create A More Positive Mindset 98
Chapter 29: How to Value Being Alone 102
Chapter 30: 8 Steps To Develop Beliefs That Will Drive you To Success 105
Chapter 31: 10 Habits of Adele 110
Chapter 32: Conflict Is Not Abuse 114
Chapter 33: 6 Ways To Be More Confident In Bed 117
Chapter 34: Happy People Celebrate Other People's Success 121
Chapter 35: 10 Habits of Serena Williams 123
Chapter 36: 8 Ways To Love Yourself First 127

Chapter 1:
20 Affirmations For Women

If you are like me you know there is only so much you can control throughout the day. What I can control is the way you think and how I perceive the world around you. Sometimes it's easy to let the stress of the world seep in and affect your mindset.

That said, with the help of positive affirmations you can improve not only your mood but your outlook on life. So in this article, I'll quickly explain the power of affirmations and give you 20 positive affirmations for women.

1. I feel the love of others who are not around me.
2. I am an amazing gift to myself, my friends, and the world. I am too much of an amazing gift to feel self-pity.
3. I love and appreciate myself. I am who I am and I love myself.
4. I do not need the company of others to feel complete. I am more than enough. I enjoy being in my own solitude.
5. The past no longer matters. It has no control over me. What only matters is the present. What I do in the present will shape my future. The past has no say in this.
6. Everything that I need will be provided to me at the right time and the right place. When something is meant to happen it will happen.
7. It is too early to give up on my dreams. it is always too early to give up on my dreams.
8. I will not give up until I have tried everything. And when I have tried everything I will look for other ways to try.

9. I believe in myself and I believe in the path I have chosen. I cannot choose the obstacles in my way, but I can choose to continue on my path, because it leads to my goals.

10. I am not only enough, I am more than enough. I also get better every day I live. Tomorrow I will be a better version of myself than I was today.

11. I will not criticize myself. I will love myself for who I am and for what I have become.

12. I will award and praise myself for my accomplishments. I will not dwell on the praise of others for my own praise is more than enough.

13. I will not compare myself to anyone else because everyone is on their own personal journeys. My journey is unique and cannot be compared.

14. I will only compare myself to myself. I know what greatness I can accomplish and I will only hold myself to that.

15. I will not look at the darkness in the world around me but instead at the light that is within me.

16. I am happy with who I am. I am happy I am in my own skin. I am enough and I do not need to be someone else.

17. The answer is always in front of me, even if I have not yet seen it. As long as I continued to search I will find the answer.

18. Every problem I ever face will have a solution. There has never been a question without an answer. I just need to discover the answer.

19. I am a smart, capable, brilliant woman, and I have everything I need to get through this. When I make it through this I will be better for it.

20. Those who love me will always love me, even if they do not fully understand my dreams. True friends and family will love me regardless of what my dreams. False friends will love me because of my dreams.

You don't need to repeat every single one of these positive affirmations throughout the course of a day. Chances are you don't have the time, and you may not need some of them (at least not currently. Instead, you need to:

- Take a few moments out of your day to breathe while repeating some of your favorite affirmations.
- Say the affirmations out loud. It works better if you hear them spoken.
- If you keep a journal you can write meaningful affirmations down. Much like saying the affirmations out loud, writing them down helps make it feel more real (than simply thinking them).
- Use the affirmations often. There's no such thing as too many affirmations.

I hope you've found some of these affirmations helpful. Give them a try. I know many have helped me over the years. And if you want to learn more about how to boost your physical and mental wellbeing make sure to check out another one of my affirmation blogs right here!

Chapter 2:
8 Ways To Gain Self-Confidence

Confidence is not something that can be inherited or learned but is rather a state of mind. Confidence is an attribute that most people would kill to possess. It comes from the feelings of well-being, acceptance of your body and mind (your self-esteem), and belief in your ability, skills, and experience. Positive thinking, knowledge, training, and talking to other people are valuable ways to help improve or boost your confidence levels. Although the definition of self-confidence is different for everyone, the simplest one can be 'to have faith and believe in yourself.'

Here are 8 Ways To Gain More Self-Confidence:

1. Look at what you have already achieved:

It's easy to lose confidence when we dwell on our past mistakes and believe that we haven't actually achieved anything yet. It's common to degrade ourselves and not see our achievements as something special. But we should be proud of ourselves even if we do just a single task throughout the day that benefited us or the society in any way. Please make a list of all the things you are proud of, and it can be as small as cleaning your room or as big as getting a good grade or excelling in your job. Keep adding your small or significant achievements every day. Whenever you feel low in confidence, pull out the list and remind yourself how far you have come, how many amazing things you have done, and how far you still have to go.

2. Polish the things you're already good at:

We feel confident in the things we know we are good at. Everyone has some kind of strengths, talents, and skills. You just have to recognize what's yours and work towards it to polish it. Some people are naturally good at everything they do. But that doesn't make you any less unique. You have to try to build on those things that you are good at, and they will help you built confidence in your abilities.

3. Set goals for yourself daily:

Whether it's cooking for yourself, reading a book, studying for a test, planning to meet a friend, or doing anything job-related, make a to-do list for yourself daily. Plan the steps that you have to take to achieve them. They don't necessarily have to be big goals; you should always aim for small achievements. At the end of the day, tick off all the things you did. This will help you gain confidence in your ability to get things done and give you a sense of self-appreciation and self-worth.

4. Talk yourself up:

That tiny voice inside of our heads is the key player in the game of our lives. You'll always be running low on confidence if that voice constantly has negative commentary in your mind telling you that you're not good enough. You should sit somewhere calm and quiet and talk to yourself out of all the negative things. Treat yourself like you would treat a loved one when they tend to feel down. Convince yourself that you can achieve anything, and there's nothing that can stop you. Fill your mind with positive thoughts and act on them.

5. **Get a hobby:**

Find yourself something that really interests you. It can either be photography, baking, writing, reading, anything at all. When you have found yourself something you are passionate about, commit yourself to it and give it a go. Chances are, you will get motivated and build skills more quickly; this will help you gain self-confidence as you would gradually get better at it and feel accomplished. The praises you will get for it will also boost your confidence.

6. **Face your fears:**

The best way to gain confidence is to face your fears head-on. There's no time to apply for a promotion or ask someone out on a date until you feel confident enough. Practice facing your fears even if it means that you will embarrass yourself or mess up. Remind yourself that it's just an experiment. You might learn that making mistakes or being anxious isn't half as bad as you would have thought. It will help you gain confidence each time you move forward, and it will prevent you from taking any risks that will result in negative consequences.

7. Surround yourself with positive people:

Observe your friends and the people around you. Do they lift you and accept who you are or bring you down and point out your flaws? A man is known by the company he keeps. Your friends should always positively influence your thoughts and attitude and make you feel better about yourself.

8. Learn To Strike A Balance:

Self-confidence is not a static measure. Some days, we might feel more confident than others. We might often feel a lack of confidence due to criticism, failures, lack of knowledge, or low self-esteem. While another time we might feel over-confident. We might come off as arrogant and self-centred to other people, and it can eventually lead to our failure. We should keep a suitable amount of confidence within ourselves.

Conclusion:

Confidence is primarily the result of how we have been taught and brought up. We usually learn from others how to behave and what to think of ourselves. Confidence is also a result of our experiences and how we learn to react in different situations. Everyone struggles with confidence issues at one time or another, but these quick fixes should enough to boost your confidence. Start with the easier targets, and then work yourself up. I believe in you. Always!

Chapter 3:
How To Use Affirmations For Success

Affirmations are best described as a self-help strategy that is used to promote self-confidence and belief in your abilities. There might come a million instances where you felt like you needed to affirm yourself, and there would be many moments when you have probably affirmed yourself without even realizing it. Simple sentences like "I've got what it takes" or "I believe in my ability to succeed" shift your focus away from the perceived inadequacies or failures and direct your focus towards your strengths. While affirmations may not be a magic bullet for instant success, they generally work as a tool for shifting your mindset and achieving your goals.

Neuroplasticity, or our brain's ability to adapt and change to different circumstances throughout our lives, makes us understand what makes affirmations work and how to make them more effective. Creating a mental image beforehand of doing something that you're scared of, like acing a nerve-wracking interview or bungee jumping to conquer your fear of heights, can encourage your brain to take these positive affirmations as fact, and soon your actions will tend to follow.

Repeating affirmations can help you boost your confidence and motivation, but you still must take some action yourself. Affirmations are a step towards the change, not the change itself. They can also help you to achieve your goals by strengthening your confidence by reminding you that you're in control of your success and what you can do right now to achieve it. Affirmations give you a list of long-standing patterns and beliefs, and it makes you act as if you've already succeeded. Understand that affirmations alone can't produce a change in every situation. You have to take some actions too along with them. Similarly, affirming your traits can also help you see yourself in a new light.

To get the most benefits from affirmations, start a regular practice and make it a habit. Say affirmations upon waking up and getting into bed; give them at least 3-5 minutes. Repeat each of your affirmations ten times, focus on the words that leave your mouth. Believe them to be true while saying them. Make it a consistent habit. You have to be patient and stick with your practice, and it might take some time before you see evident changes. Practicing affirmations can also activate the reward system in your brain, which can impact how you experience both emotional and physical pain. The moment you start managing your stress and other life difficulties, it would help you promote faith in yourself and boost self-empowerment.

Chapter 4:
When It Is Time To Slow Down

Go faster. Do more. Hustle. Hustle even more. Sound familiar? Social media is full of influencers, entrepreneurs, and "gurus" touting the virtues of hustling at all costs. It's reached the point where hustling, and even just talking about hustling, appears to be more important that actually producing results. People confuse "hustling" with "productivity" and mistake "working" for "results." They don't have a mindfulness practice. They didn't make time for trips, fun, friends, or family. They think that if they worked harder, and worked more hours, they'd be more successful. That is not true if all you do is work, work work. You will be burnt out.

The antidote to the "always hustling" mindset is "slowness." It sounds crazy, but slowing down can be the difference between success or failure, or between thriving and burning out. While more and more personal coaches and social-media influencers, qualified or not, tout the hustle lifestyle, successful leaders and entrepreneurs who actually create results in their lives know that slowing down builds the foundation for their success. Here are four reasons why slowing down can actually help you accelerate your success, enjoy a deeper sense of fulfillment, and create the life you want.

1. What's the point of hustling if you're going in the wrong direction? Too many people work tirelessly down a path that won't give them the results they want. It's like running on a treadmill...you're working, but you're not going anywhere. Slow down and make time for clarity. You can't see where you're going if you're too busy running with your head down.

2. If your goal is to succeed, then you should be willing to take the time to honor what your mind, body, and spirit need to stay healthy. When every day provides 24 hours, there's really no excuse not to meditate, exercise, cook a healthy meal, or journal.

3. Too many people fail to see the benefits in their emotions. Emotions are a guide, and they help you take inventory of what's happening in and around you, and how best to respond. Successful people feel and manage their emotions, and they don't let them trigger bad behaviors or actions. There's a mantra that sums this up well: If you can name it, you can tame it. By slowing down, you can feel the emotions you're experiencing and describe them. In doing so, you can process them and let them guide you to a healthy response.

4. What good is hustling all the time if a single decision can undo all the work you invested? To put it simply, your mind is like a

car engine: If you always have your pedal to the floor, the engine will redline, overheat, and fail. When you slow down and make time for rest and meditation, you lower your baseline for mental stress. When your mind isn't racing, it's free to absorb information, assess the circumstances, and make a good decision. If success requires making good decisions, and slowing down helps you make better decisions, then consider how you can invest more time in slowing down.

Consider the benefits described above and identify one simple step toward bringing more slowness into your life. See how that goes, and then try more. As someone who hustled himself into a concussion and changed, I can tell you that life is much better when you balance the hustle with slowness.

Chapter 5: What Are You Measuring In Your Life?

Do you know your long game? Do you know what is that single thing that you want to keep for a long time? Do you have the simple and straight process to keep your life on track? What is it that you are searching for in your life?

You see, we all are living our lives in certain ways. We all are having a routine that suites us individually. But we don't know if we are actually making a change in our life or not!

Take this for an example. You are hired by a company as a senior manager. You work in that company for a year or so. You are following all the basic duties required of you. You have notable respect that comes with your position. But on what metrics can you say that this respect is what people give you for your dedicated word and not because you are someone's boss.

We might be earning a lot of money, but we cannot say for sure that we have everything we want in life. We might be making wealth upon wealth but we cannot ensure happiness and satisfaction in our life.

So what are we earning in our life for real? What is it that we want to do that will make us look back and smile for everything that happened to us because of some smart decisions?

So start counting today! Take notes for everything even remotely quantifiable!

Numbers aren't just random figures, but they can be a source of satisfaction when we see a rise in certain cases.

You want to look out for newer ways to keep and grow the excitement in life where you don't have to work continuously and deliberately for good results, but your regular activities keep the cycles going.

Take this for an example. If you are relying on people to make you happy, or if you are falsifying the true numbers and manipulating the opinions. You are at great risk of being stripped off of all the real respect you might have ever had.

You can be the New York Times Best Seller. You can be the Best Seller on Amazon but, it will matter to you in the long game of life if you did all that with raw effort and raw ratings of your average reader.

You cannot have a happy life unless you have had a life full of adversity. You cannot be truly sure of everything unless you have gone through everything.

There are a lot of other things in life too, that are much more important than any other aspect of our lives. Things like Love, Morality, Purpose of life, and meaning for everything that we end up doing.

These things need to be measured but the harder we try, the more we end up hurting someone else who is emotionally attached to us.

So keep a check of your environment for the things that matter to you the most, because you and only you will be the best judge of that trait and that other person in your life.

Chapter 6:
<u>Don't Live Your Life In Regret</u>

Take this for a lesson today; There is no greater pain than that of regret.

Hopelessness is one thing that can crack a soul, but nothing is more hurting than that of lifelong regret. We take up things in our life that we deem helpful for the times to come. But never do we ever take risks, just because we want to have a smooth uncomplicated life.

Life was never meant to be lived as reading off a paper. Neither can you expect it to be a smooth walk on a beach? There are always some pebbles on the way and always some hedges where you need to twist and turn to fit and climb.

We all will eventually o through a period of endless questioning where we judge our every step and every decision whether if it was bad or not good enough!

But why are we indulging in this waste of time when we have so much better things to do right now in this present time slot.

When you are on a long journey, nothing will make sense. When you are on your path to greatness, you will always look back and get drawn back a little every time.

But once you reach the top, you will have a final look back into your past and everything will make sense in a split second.

Life is a roller coaster and we all have baggage. We must have because no one can have lived a long life and have a straight, plain, and colorless script where nothing happened out of the ordinary.

The uncertainty of life is what defines life to its true reality.

We, humans, are a combination of deterministic and non-deterministic behavior where we get triggered on thoughts of shame and failure but rarely do we learn to listen to those failures and try to change our habits.

Things have a course of happening and we always get behind the things that take most of us down the lane. That is where we feel the walk of shame and remember the feeling for the rest of our life.

But why do we feel the urge to remain connected to our shameful past? What needs do we have with feeling shame? Why do we need to remember and regret the things that the world has forgotten a long time ago? Why do we need to keep those memories alive?

A billion incidents are happening every second and we try to keep all our baggage with us till the day we take it with us to our graves.

What we should be doing is to forgive everyone and especially ourselves, to release some positive energy and make some space for the happy times that are to come.

We should let those happy moments erase all our regrets and ease our path for the best future that time could ever earn us. But what you should do ultimately, is to regret what you haven't done yet, rather than what you have done!

Chapter 7:
Why nobody cares when you fail

In a world this big, it is hard for everyone to care about others. We all have a busy life; we have thousands of things to do before we go to bed. Everybody focuses on themselves and is trying to make their life better. So when anyone around us wins, their success makes the noise, and people notice that. Like when you sit in an interview, nobody will see how many times you have failed, but they will see that there is a reason that you are sitting in that interview.

The main reason why nobody cares if you fail is that everyone has a life of their own, and they can't just think or care about your failure for your whole life; sure, they would try to comfort you, but eventually, they will have to go back to their own lives, and they wouldn't care about your failure anymore, now they can't be blamed for this because it is simply human nature to resume their own lives.

People don't care about your failure, I mean, of course, your family and friends would, but others wouldn't because failures don't excite them; however insensitive it may sound to you, but it is the truth. People prefer to listen to success stories that excite them and, above all, motivate them.

The people themselves need someone to give them hope that one day they can also become a success, but nobody wants to care about failures; they would rather care about your success, so don't give up just yet because if they don't care now, they will care later. "Life is hard" we all have heard this, but this hits differently when we fail, but failures are not something to be afraid of; in this life, you can't always win; sometimes, you need to fail to gain success.

And honestly, what can people even do if you fail? Nobody can give you a happy and good life, and only you can make yourself a success. Failing is not a bad thing; it is something that no one can avoid, so when you fail, and you think that nobody cares, think for a second that maybe these people have also been through the same, and they know how it feels when people acknowledge your failures. People prefer to have a person they can call a hero, and they like to hear the stories of that hero and his success; even when the hero fails, nobody cares about his failure because they prefer to mind their own business when something like that happens.

Everyone is too focused on their own life, their own goals, and their failures to care about someone else's failures because they would rather care about their lives than yours, so don't take it negatively; it is okay if they don't care, use that to your advantage and work on yourself, now is the time to work hard and be successful and once your successful everyone will care.

The only thing you can do is forget about the people and remember yourself, remember that everyone who is a hero now has failed more than twice, so don't go thinking why they don't care because everyone has problems that they are worried about now and that is the reason they don't care. The only thing you should remember is that you should never give up because "Success comes from failures."

Chapter 8:
6 Ways To Achieve Peak Performance

To be successful requires much more than just your intelligence and talent. There are basic needs which have to be met to function at your peak. These basic needs are neglected by most, impairing their capacity to rise to those elusive higher levels of success and happiness in life.

1. Get enough sleep

Sleep deprivation means peak performance deprivation. Without proper sleep you wake up to meet the day feeling scatterbrained, foggy and unfocused. You grab your cup of coffee to get a charge on your brain, which completely depletes your brain function over the course of the day, making your brain even more exhausted.

Good sleep improves your ability to be patient, retain information, think clearly, make good decisions and be present and alert in all your daily interactions. Sleep is your time off from problem solving.

When you get the proper rest your brain becomes awake, alive and ready to generate the cognitive prowess and emotional regulation you need to function at your peak performance.

2. Drink lemon water

Lemon water is a great substitute for your morning coffee. Although lemons do not contain caffeine, lemon water has excellent pick-me-up properties without negative side effects. It energizes the brain, especially if it is warm, and hydrates your lymph system.

Among the most important benefits of lemon water are its strong antibacterial, antiviral, and immune-boosting power, making sick days from work nearly non-existent. Lemon water cures headache, freshens breath, cleanses the skin, improves digestion, eliminates PMS with its diuretic properties and reduces the acidity in the body.

Most importantly, lemon water increases your cognitive capacity and improves mood with its stimulating properties on the brain, helping you to operate more consistently in your peak performance zone.

3. Get daily exercise

Exercise is the best way to reduce the stress that impairs your performance stamina. Exercise increases your "happy" mood chemicals through the release of endorphins. Endorphins help rid your mind and body of tension alleviating anxiety helping you to calm down.

The brain needs physical activity to stay flexible. Exercise stimulates neurogenesis, or the growth of new brain cells, which improves overall brain function. The development of new brain cells keeps your brain young and in shape, allowing you to be more efficient, pliable and clear in your decision making, higher thinking and learning capacities. Neurogenesis is the catalyst to peak performance.

Further, there is nothing that can bring down self-esteem quicker than not liking how you look. Exercise improves self-confidence and your perception of your attractiveness and self-worth. This confidence contributes greatly to your success, prompting people to respect you and take you seriously

4. Have emotional support

Having healthy, loving relationships increases your happiness, success and longevity by promoting your capacity to function in life as your best self. Social connectedness and love gives you relationships to be motivated for and people to be inspired by.

A strong social network decreases stress, provides you with a sense of belonging and gives your life the deeper meaning it needs. When you are loved and loving, and carving out quality time to cultivate these relationships, you are exalted, elevated and encouraged to live your dreams fully.

5. Be unapologetically optimistic

A requirement of peak performance is to look for the best in every situation. Optimism is the commitment to believe, expect and trust that things in life are rigged in your favor. Even when something bad happens, you find the silver lining.

A positive outlook on life strengthens your immune system and the emotional quality of your life experiences, allowing you to be resilient in the face of fear, stress and challenge.

Being an optimist or a pessimist boils down to the way you talk to yourself. When you are optimistic you are fierce in the belief it is your own actions which result in positive things happening. You live by positive affirmation, take responsibility for your own happiness and anticipate more good things will happen for you in the future.

When bad things happen you do not blame yourself, you are simply willing to change yourself.

6. Have time alone

Time alone is refueling to your physical, mental, emotional and spiritual self. This time recharges you, helping to cultivate your peak performance levels again and again. You must give yourself time to recover from the stress of consistently being around others. Being around people continuously wears down your ability to regulate your emotional state, causing self-regulation fatigue. For this reason you must give yourself permission to take the pressure off and disconnect.

Chapter 9:
11 Ways To Attract Love

The following ideas are to attract **true love** and romance into your life. These fun and practical little tips will magnify your energy and get the Law of Attraction sending more love your way whether you're single or need a little spark in your relationship.

1. Get Specific: What Kind Of A Relationship Would You Like In Your Life?

Take out a piece of paper or open up a document on your computer and list out what kind of relationship you would like to have in your life. *What does it look like? How does it work? Will you get married?* Get specific. God/The Universe/Source Energy is always in the details.

2. Let Go Of Your Past, De-Clutter And Move Forward

This means not talking about 'him or her' as much and perhaps getting rid of old love letters or emails that keep you stuck in the past. It's time to pave the way for a new person to step forward. They can't arrive when you're still pining over someone else.

3. Watch Movies Of The Love You Would Like To Attract

Without a doubt 'The Notebook' is the romantic movie that most people refer to when they think of the type of love they would like to attract. Go to IMDB and search for romantic movies and create a 'must watch list'.

4. Show Yourself The Love You Think You Deserve

It's really important to know how good (or not so good) your levels of self-esteem are. You really need to love yourself in order to attract a relationship that is sustainable. The truth? Otherwise you'll be attracting someone that will want to fix you or will magnify your need to take care of yourself better. This can be a good thing, but unless you shine light on the need for self-love and self-care then it can turn ugly very fast. So this is why it's so important to treat yourself well and show yourself the love you think you deserve.

How will you love yourself today? Ask yourself this powerful question at least 3 times per day.

5. Buy Yourself Flowers Or Tickets To Something You Want To Watch

Surrounding yourself with bunches of fresh and beautiful blooms is a great way to raise your vibration. It encapsulates the essence of springtime and is really lovely and feminine. Also take yourself on a date to the movies. Watch something that you really want to see. This is an act of strengthening levels of self love.

6. Create Space In Your Bedroom For Your Lover

I learnt this one from 'The Game of Life and How to Play It' where Florence Scovel Shinn writes about the importance of demonstrating something called 'active faith'. It's where you create space for whatever it is that you wish to welcome in your life. By creating space in your bedroom for your lover you are letting the Universe know that you're ready. You can do this by just sleeping on one side of the bed, making drawer space available for his or her clothes.

7. Soul Mate Journal Exercise

Write a clear list of all of the things you would like to do with your soul mate. List out the dates, tourist attractions, events and fun things you can do together. Feel excited about sharing these experiences with someone.

8. Crystal Magic

Get some rose quartz to flow energy into and use it as an attraction point for manifesting love. Carry it with you as a reminder of the lover that is on track to find you soon.

9. Buy A Special Dinner Plate For Your Lover Or A Coffee Cup

Imagine making a cup of tea or coffee for your lover each morning. By buying a special cup you can visualize the process of having him/her there with you. The Universe will respond to this action.

10. Feel Energized When You See Others In Love

Don't be one of those people that see public displays of affection or people blissfully in love and allow it to activate your crabby/skeptical mind. You can only attract success when you are genuinely happy for others and their success. Allow yourself to be energized by the love that others share and affirm to yourself that your time is on its way very soon.

11. Read Some Rumi Poems

"The minute I heard my first love story,
I started looking for you, not knowing
how blind that was.

Chapter 10:
20 More Positive Affirmations

A positive affirmation is a statement about yourself that is phrased in the positive, present tense. It reflects an area of your life, emotions, or belief system that you want to improve or change. The potential benefits of affirmations are vast. Positive affirmations empower you to become the best version of yourself. They inspire you to act in ways that help you fulfill your potential. You can use positive affirmations to reprogram negative thoughts into positive beliefs. The ability to reprogram your beliefs about yourself has the potential to transform your life completely.

For an affirmation to be effective, it needs to meet four criteria.

Each positive affirmation you use should be:

1. **Worded in the present tense**
2. **Positive**
3. **Specific**
4. **Personal**

You can create your own positive affirmations using this four-step framework. The benefits of affirmations are dramatically increased when you have created it yourself from an existing negative belief. Let's say you had a belief that you are unsuccessful in your job. Where focus goes, energy flows. If you keep feeding this belief, it will manifest as truth.

When you understand this, you can see how our thoughts really do shape our reality. Instead, you can use this belief as an opportunity to grow. Take that statement and switch it to its positive opposite. Rather than thinking: 'I am terrible at my job, I'll never get a promotion, my boss hates me,' you now think 'I am great at my job, I love what I do, and I always put 100% effort into every task

Whether you choose to formulate your own positive affirmations or use the ones I have created for you below, you must cultivate a daily practice. The best times to practice are first thing in the morning and last thing at night (or whenever you feel that you need to repeat them to start feeling better). During these times, your mind is more open and will absorb the statements on a deeper level.

It is best if you say them out loud while looking in the mirror. Speaking them to yourself affirms that you trust in yourself, and you believe the statements to be true. If speaking them out loud is not possible, you can say them in your mind. Writing them out a few times a week is also beneficial. Try getting a journal specifically for this purpose. Another technique that you might find useful is to pin the written affirmations to the mirror or refrigerator, where you will see them often.

When you are just beginning with this practice, it may be easy to forget, so set an alert on your phone or in your calendar to remind you. Here are 20 examples of positive affirmations relating to different areas of life.

Choose the ones that resonate most with you. Once you feel that you have integrated those particular statements, you can select or create new ones for other areas you want to improve.

Confidence and Self-Esteem

1: "I feel confident in every situation."

2: "I like who I am."

3: "I am a good person."

4: "I am great at helping people."

5: "I feel valued by my friends and family."

Inner Strength and Resilience

1: "I meet each new challenge with enthusiasm."

2: "I am strong and stable."

3: "I think I can, so I can."

4: "No matter what happens, I can handle it."

5: "I am powerful."

Positivity and Joy

1: **"I radiate joy to everyone I meet."**

2: **"I see the best in people."**

3: **"In the present moment there are no issues, only peace."**

4: **"Happiness is a choice; today, I choose to be happy."**

5: **"I have the power to turn negative thoughts into positive beliefs."**

Career and Success

1: **"I deserve success."**

2: **"I can succeed at whatever I choose."**

3: **"I am good at my job, and I love what I do."**

4: **"I have great ideas."**

5: **"I am innovative and tenacious."**

I hope that my guide to positive affirmations for men has provided you with a solid foundation for designing your perfect practice. Remember, to reap the benefits of affirmations, you should say them out loud every day and write them out a few times a week. Use any of my examples of positive affirmations, or for extra power, try creating your own using my framework. If you commit to a daily practice, you will soon notice the benefits in your career, relationships, emotional resilience, sense of self-worth, and confidence.

Chapter 11:
Stop Wasting Time on the Details and Commit to the Fundamentals

Time runs on a treadmill that has no apparent switch. We have a timeline on this planet and it will come to an end sooner or later. It would be sooner than we think, that is for sure!

But what we put in, to live what time we have to make it matter for if it were our last second, is a concept I'll try to endorse here.

You see, we all live our lives as if no one is more sincere and dedicated than we are. We put in all the hours and we put in all the energy but we can't guarantee anything, can we?

It is never about how hardworking you are. It is never about the rules and the intricacies of things we follow. It is never about the hours we put in, but what we put into the hours!

This is not as simple as it may sound. We, humans, have a common flaw as an intelligent species. It is an adherent flaw in our upbringing and the norms that we follow.

We don't know what is more important, is it the plane or the pilot? We have what we call an instinctive nature that draws us to conclusions and things that will influence us to ultimately find our purpose, but in that process of finding one, we lose focus of what we have at hand right now!

We are working straight hours for things that have secondary importance in our lives and sometimes can be discouraging. We are working so hard on things that have least to no contribution to our happiness and success but we are still going on around them foolishly.

Not everything is meant to be done and not everything is meant to bring meaning to the spice of life. But we still do it because we are naive and shallow.

We need to learn what are the fundamentals of living a successful life.

You don't have a single aspect of your life to take care of. You can't dedicate the majority of your time and attention to fixing only one thing when there are a lot more and lot better things to take care of.

You don't need to avoid the bigger and bolder realities just because you are afraid you might fail and fall. You surely can and you surely will. You only have to keep trying and you will eventually set things straight.

Set your priorities in the right direction. You don't need a fancy logo for your business if you haven't had a single paying customer yet. You can't have a better grade if you haven't done any of the term work. You can't expect to be paid a full wager if you have dozens of chores still pending for the next day.

The details are useless if you haven't had the fundamentals done yet. The final formula has no meaning if you had the basic equation wrong. So follow the process and the process will lead you to the final viewpoint!

Chapter 12:
When It's Okay to Not Be Okay

Let's be honest, happiness is not something you can "just choose". If It was, then sad moments could not be there. Do not pressure yourself to be happy, because if you do, then you are inadvertently setting a path of the war with yourself. This is why **adopting a mindset that embraces** "not all that happy" feelings we can arise within us is essential for carrying on with a happier life.

In the stumbling on happiness, Daniel Gilbert describes happiness, "There is no basic recipe for happiness." Certainly, it's anything but an objective to accomplish. Or maybe it's the bi-result of carrying on with a wholehearted life - a daily existence wherein we permit ourselves to chance feel the full range of human feeling - dissatisfaction, grief, dismissal, misery, insufficiency - and to accept our battles and to acknowledge our ourselves as the questionable "human becoming" that we are".

We can help ourselves along in that cycle by accomplishing a greater amount of what grows our ability for every one of the encounters and feelings that life holds available.
Here are a 7 Ways To help You Cope and Accept When It's Okay Not to Be Okay.

1. **Accept Life's Upsetting Emotions.**

Bear this in mind, there are only two types of people who don't usually experience painful emotions; psychopaths and people who've died. Feeling or experiencing sad and painful moments are part and parcel of your life. At any point when you deny, excuse, numb or attempt to obstruct yourself from feeling them completely – something many are profoundly adroit at doing – you are just prolonging your torment and making superfluous suffering.

2. **Practice "gently/friendly curiosity"**

As human beings, the truth is, we are intrinsically emotional or passionate creatures– occasionally, we act before reasoning. Also, satisfaction – those sentiments bliss, happiness, and connection - is only one of the numerous feelings on the wide enthusiastic range.

The best way to encounter unadulterated snapshots of happiness, connection, appreciation, and love is the point at which you allow yourself to experience sadness, misery, dread, and hurt. Embrace these sad feelings with curiosity. This requires allowing yourself to sit with the less lovely feelings without desensitizing, minimizing, or over-relating to them. As such, "the solitary way out is through."

3. **Practice More of Whatever Makes You Stronger – Body, Mind, and Soul.**

Since numerous things in your life are out of your control, it bodes well to be proactive in those parts of your life over which we have some proportion of control. Growing day by day customs and propensities to assist you with bringing your "best self" to your greatest difficulties is vital. Eat well, burn some calories, invest your energy with individuals who lift you. Limit time with the individuals who don't. Re-energize your energy, re-focus your soul, and pull together on your first concerns. The little private every day moves you make can lead to large open outcomes that you frequently need.

4. Look at Yourself as a Person Who Is "Human Becoming"

Every time you will see people who seem to have everything in perfect order, and feel they don't encounter any of the battles and uncertainties that you do. It's untrue.

Accepting yourself as a 'human becoming that you are – complete with every one of your inadequacies, fears, and frailty – helps you to grow fully into your humankind and connect all more with that of others.

Everyone at some point in their lives messes up, falls down and up, and fails to be as kind-hopeful patient-restrained as they'd prefer to be. Such is the human condition. Thumping yourself for being human doesn't serve you. This is the reason, in your fallen moments, you should be kinder to yourself. Commit to accepting your flaws or imperfections and acknowledge your mistakes as you move up to healing.

5. Rest Your Sadness

Thinking of sadness as the opposite of happiness is easy, and accordingly, something to be evaded. Truth be told, misery is the feeling that directs you toward what you care about most and is a pathway to happiness. At the point when you cut yourself off from feeling the profundity of your misfortune, from sitting with your misery and distress, you additionally cut yourself off from being available to bliss, close connection, and happiness.

Therefore, allowing yourself ample time to sit with your sadness, let the tears flow-if need be, and be there fully to feel the sad moments-that permitting yourself to fully feel the ache -taking all things together in its rawness - allows you to gradually discover your way back wholly and healing and to getting more deliberate in your work, as a parent, and throughout everyday life. It's an excursion that is continuous.

6. Cultivate Seeds of Gratitude

Happiness cannot be bought from external sources, be it money, success, and fame. It is all on everyone's knowledge that most people who are materially wealthy are profoundly unhappy. Which is true. You should learn to appreciate whatever you have, hence the more appreciation, the happier you will feel. It's the reason we must be purposeful in zeroing in on the things that fuel feelings of appreciation, in any event, when there are parts of our lives that aren't as we'd like.

7. Spend your time offline-take a break from social media

Finally, perhaps the main thing you can do to cultivate happiness and develop your versatility for managing your afflictions is being in a place where there are meaningful relationships. Turning to the right people and connecting with them in realness and during your vulnerable moments is more impactful on your inner peace instead of scrolling down the social media feeds.

In conclusion, it is okay to be vulnerable- it is okay to feel unhappy-it is okay to share the feeling with the right people. Just keep in mind that an unhappy feeling which is felt enough can permanently reside in your psyche and overshadow all others. So, feel what should be felt and afterward be deliberate in investing your time and attention toward whatever re-establishes viewpoint and grows your ability to make a move to make whatever it is you need a greater amount of in your life.

Chapter 13:
How To Deal With Impatience

"The big challenge with impatience is that it's largely justifiable. The way you respond, however, may not be." - Matt Christensen.

Why is he talking so loudly? Why is she walking so slowly? Why isn't he doing his chores? We have all been hit with the impatient nerve now and then. Although these situations aren't avoidable, how we deal and communicate with them counts in the end. The impatience that vibrates through our body can easily make us angry or result in other unpleasant reactions. It can get triggered by a phrase, behavior, or task that often stems from strength, anxiety, or related outside factors. Becoming more patient takes more time.

Dealing with impatience is surely hectic, but it's not that difficult once you master some techniques. The first thing to do when you're being impatient is to take several deep breaths. Our brains tend to go into a fight or flight situation whenever they sniff danger. As a result, hyperventilation or shortage of oxygen occurs. You start getting more excited and stressed and take quick, short breaths that do more harm than good. The best solution is to give yourself time and take a few seconds to breathe deeply. Catch your impatience with a productive response by calming and controlling your mind and body.

The next thing after relaxing your mind is to relax your muscles. When you feel impatient, give attention to your muscles by doing progressive muscle relaxation. Sit comfortably in a position and meditate. Stretch your arms and legs, and then stretch all of your tensed points one by one. Try to relax as much as you can. You will end up feeling calm, and the feeling of impatience will vanish.

We have all heard how communication is the key to dealing with almost everything. It can be fulfilling and productive to speak up about what's making you impatient and what's bothering you. But beware! It would help if you practiced tact and finesse to make sure you don't sound like a jerk when talking about your impatience-ness. Voicing your views out loud is an essential step in combating impatience. Acknowledging your feelings would also open doors for you to ask for help.

Impatience also thrives on disconnection. If not given the appropriate validation, it can be a recipe for a meltdown. Validation, both verbal and non-verbal responses, can communicate understanding, which can further facilitate connection. Validation can taper your impatience by helping shape your behavior and communication.

Dwelling on the feeling of being impatient can get you nowhere. It doesn't provide you with any sense of productiveness, helpfulness, or pleasantness. Rather than being caught up in the immediate goal, we must keep reminding ourselves to keep a larger perspective of the situation.

Always be mindful of your situations and trust your instinct to deal with your problems. Some people become impatient because of underlying unresolved issues, such as anger, perfectionism, and depression/anxiety. Try helping yourself with acceptance and commitment therapy, anger management, or CBT if you think you are caught up in these feelings. Remember, being patient can get you so many places, while being impatient will have you stuck in one!

Chapter 14:
6 Habits of Strong Couples

Relationships don't always come with guaranteed success. They are always a risk for those who choose to fall in love with each other. People open themselves up to the possibilities of heartbreak and getting hurt whenever things don't go their way. They make so much effort and invest a considerable part of themselves into the relationship in the hopes of not getting emotionally betrayed in the end. Relationships can be stressful and difficult to bear, and the couple's habits can have a powerful impact on the relationship. We can either create positive or negative habits, but once we start practicing them, they will eventually become a part of our unconscious act.

Research says that it takes us 21 days to develop a habit, whether positive or negative. When it comes to having a healthy and happy relationship, certain habits can have a positive and powerful impact. Here are some healthy habits that you need to practice every day to become second nature to you and help you build a stronger connection with your partner.

1. Always Show Mutual Respect

Respecting your partner is a crucial ingredient for creating a healthy, happy, and long-lasting connection. It is a habit that is worth developing. Expressing respect towards your partner shows your love, acceptance, and warmth towards them. It shows that you value your partner, no matter the differences. Even if you both have a different outlook on life, you mustn't disrespect your partner or put them down. This goes both ways. If your partner disagrees with you, they should show respect towards you. It's not about both of you not agreeing on a situation, but rather how you handle the issue as a team that makes all the difference in the world.

2. Communicate With Each Other

Communication is perhaps an essential quality of a healthy relationship. But there are instances when we can't communicate appropriately with our partners or come off as emotionally unavailable to them. But healthy and happy couples have this game down. They vocalize their feelings and love for each other and offer compliments and gestures. And instead of sweeping the issues under the rug, they discuss all the bad and negative stuff that bothers them. No matter how awkward or uncomfortable you both might feel, it's always essential to talk about your feelings to move forward and grow.

3. Spending Some Time Apart

As much as it is vital to spend time together with your partner, it's equally important to spend it apart. Being able to be independent and doing your stuff is critical in any relationship. You cannot always depend on your partner for things that you can easily do yourself. Spending too much time together can create unhealthy codependency. Both of them should maintain healthy boundaries and autonomy to ensure a long-lasting relationship.

4. Love Languages

Gary Chapman came up with the concept that men and women have five love languages. They can either be words of affirmation, receiving gifts, quality time, acts of service, and physical touch. You and your partner need to know which love language suits you both the best. It will help both of you feel loved and stay connected with each other. Furthermore, you must attend to your partner's love language constantly.

5. Appreciate Each Other

We often forget to let our partners know that we appreciate them and don't show them much affection and appreciation. We might have it in our mind, but we fail to express and deliver it to them. But it's always important to show your significant other how much you love and appreciate them and their efforts. This could also be done through words, cards, flowers, acts of kindness, and more.

6. Say Sorry and Mean It

Partners step on each other's toes all the time, whether in big or small ways. It might be a disagreement, argument, or a fight, but recognizing your role in your partner's pain is essential. No matter who is at fault, both of you should aim for an apology that expresses empathy, takes responsibility for your wrongdoings, and shows that you're striving to change your behavior.

Conclusion

Relationships always require time, patience, and love but also healthy habits. It's easier to fall for someone and promise them the world. But if you want to make your relationship long-lasting, efforts are always required. Sometimes, the proper habits are all we need to make what we have with our partners

Chapter 15:
Why Getting Started Is More Important Than Succeeding

Our world is becoming more and more obsessed with comparison and validation. The style of thinking that is becoming dangerously common is "if you can't be number one or number two, then you might as well not play at all."

(this belief was celebrated in my mba program, which may or may not surprise you.)

But according to davenport, you don't need to be a professional to learn the most important lessons in sports. You just need to bust your butt as an athlete, regardless of the level you're playing at. I'd say it's that way in the rest of life as well. Mastering your craft isn't nearly as important as pushing yourself.

To put it another way, you'll learn more from the process of pursuing excellence than from the products of achieving it.

It's More Important To Start Than To Succeed

What if the choice to be curious was all that was required to become smarter, stronger, and more skilled? What if the willingness to try something new, even if it felt uncomfortable, was all that it took to start the slow march towards greatness?

- Are you curious enough to get in the gym and try it, even if you'll look stupid?
- Are you willing to be vulnerable and put your skin in the game to start your own business?
- Are you eager enough to improve your work that you'll battle through the frustration of producing something mediocre?

It all boils down to this: whether you'll end up being the best or the worst, are you willing to start?

The more i look at things this way, the more i believe that the willingness to start is the littlest thing in life that makes the biggest difference.

Step onto the field. Stand up in the meeting. Raise your hand in class.

Get under the bar. Walk up to the podium. Ask the first question.

Take a risk, get started, and contribute something. To your team, to your family, to your job, to your community. Whether or not you end up being number one in the world is irrelevant. Most of the time, the value you provide isn't nearly as important as pushing yourself to provide it. This is especially true at first.

Having the courage to get started is more important than succeeding because the people who consistently get started are the only ones who can end up finishing anything.

Get Started: Life Isn't A Dres's Rehearsal

I often write about what it means to live a healthy life.

I can't think of any skill more critical to the active pursuit of a healthy life than the willingness to start. Everything that signifies a happy, healthy and fulfilled existence — strong relationships, vibrant creativity, valuable work, a physical lifestyle, etc. — it all requires a willingness to get started over and over again.

Take note: being the best isn't required to be happy or fulfilled, but being in the game is necessary.

Life isn't a dress rehearsal. Only one person lives in the spotlight, but everyone benefits from stepping on stage.

Which stage will you step onto? What game will you play? How will you get started?

Chapter 16:

10 Habits of Nancy Pelosi

You can't acknowledge prominent women in the history of American politics without mentioning Nancy Pelosi. Nancy Pelosi is a well-known American politician and a Democrat. She is the current Speaker of the House of representatives for yet another term under President Biden's administration-which marks nearly 50-years in politics.

Pelosi began her political journey in 1976 when she was elected to the Democratic Party National Committee. In 1977, she rose to become the party's leader in California. Pelosi has held the positions of Minority Whip and Minority Leader. Curious of how she rose to such prominence?

Here are 10 Habits of Nancy Pelosi.

1. Establish and Pursue Your Dreams

According to Pelosi, you can't succeed in life without a clear vision and willingness to pursue it. Looking at her political career journey, it's evidence that she has achieved what she desired as a successful politician. Pelosi noted in an interview that you would fail to realize your goals if your focus is on things that don't align with your desires.

2. It Doesn't Matter What Gender You Are

Pelosi believes that it makes no difference whether you are a man or a woman; as long as you have the necessary skills, you can flourish in any role. She urges women to be courageous enough to challenge the notion of "male dominated roles." Pelosi joined politics when patriarchy was at its core and later became the first female Speaker of the House of Representatives.

3. Work Collaboratively With Others

Pelosi acknowledges the essence of working with other people who has the same affiliation as you-in this case, her democrat party members. To achieve great things, you will need the help and input of others, particularly those with more skills and experience. However, it would be best if you only worked with those who believe in you.

4. Be Your Own Best Sensationalist

Self-promotion is something frowned about, but someone has to do it. Do you know who doesn't hold back when it comes to bragging about how terrific she is? Pelosi herself. At a press conference in 2017, Pelosi flaunted how she was a master legislator, strategic, politically adept leader, among others. If you don't publicize yourself out there, who will?

5. Enjoy the Fight

There are two-way contented warriors in DC, and then there is Nancy Pelosi. In an interview, when asked to respond to Dianne Feinstein's statement that women in politics should be prepared to take a punch, she responded with a broad smile, "you must also know how to throw it too."

6. Keep Your Frenemies Closer

According to Pelosi, keep your frenemies closer enough to cooperate with when necessary. However, there is a dark, cold place for democrats like Rep. Moulton for his efforts to oust Pelosi earlier in 2018. "What do you call someone who seems 99% loyal? Disloyal!" In short, if you're going after Pelosi, you better win.

7. Be True to Your Authentic Self

When should you change your mind, and when should you stick to your guns? The answer to that all-time leadership question is not only "it depends," but also when it's right in the eyes of the public. Nancy demonstrates as she puts it, "sticking to your guns and not succumbing to needless pressure."

8. Money Talks

Money is power in politics and business; you must master the money game, as Pelosi has. Her political career has been defined by fundraising, both for her party and for individual candidates too. This is how you win hearts and list up your political allies.

9. Claim Your Place at the Table

Having spent years paddling up the ladder, expect no rush in endorsing Pelosi's replacement. As Molly Ball's book, "Pelosi" indicates, calling herself a "transitional leader" merely meant that those who wished to limit her term were naive. Did it just prove true? She exemplifies what it looks like when a woman doesn't care what other people think or call her—as long as you call her "madam speaker" one more time.

10. Leadership Is About Personal Experience

Consider this: politicians and toddlers have a lot in common, don't they? For Pelosi, having a large family and a leader necessitates being efficient with your time and getting things done. And also being patient enough when dealing with people who can throw tantrums and need to be taken care of.

Conclusion

Strong, powerful women like Nancy Pelosi demonstrates the importance of women's involvement in political processes. As a woman, embrace your power and value your experience enough to conquer a political battle that men take privilege in.

Chapter 17:
Happy People Don't Hold on To Grudges

Holding a grudge is when you harbor anger, bitterness, resentment, or other negative feelings long after someone has done something to hurt you. Usually, it's in response to something that's already occurred. Other times a grudge may develop after simply perceiving that someone is against you or means you harm—whether or not they do. Grudges also often feature persistent rumination about the person and/or incident at the center of your ill-will.

While we don't often like to admit it, holding a grudge is a common way some people respond to the feeling that they've been wronged. If you're still mad well after a precipitating incident, you may be holding on to those negative feelings for too long, sometimes well after other people typically would have let them go. You may remember multiple past bad acts and relive those experiences every time you think about or interact with that person—either making your displeasure abundantly clear to them or keeping your true feelings to yourself. You might be intentionally holding a grudge, but sometimes you aren't even aware of it.

But whatever your intentions or the cause of your bitterness, holding a grudge can end up hurting you as much as the person who inspired it. Learn more about how clinging to anger can impact you emotionally, physically, and socially, as well as how to begin to let go of your grudges and cope with anger more healthily. From early childhood on, holding a grudge is one-way people respond to negative feelings and events. This reaction is particularly common when you think someone has done something intentionally, callously, or thoughtlessly to hurt you, especially if they don't seem to care or make an attempt to apologize or make the situation right.

If you have low self-esteem, poor coping skills, were embarrassed by the hurt, and/or have a short temper, you may be even more likely to hold a grudge. While we all may fall into holding an occasional grudge, some people may be more prone to hanging on to resentments or anger than other people. Sometimes, holding grudges—and blaming others—may be a form of self-protection. In the same vein, some people may be more conscious that they are stoking feelings of bitterness than others, which may be unaware of their role in keeping their anger alive. Lasting bitterness can grow from a variety of issues—large and small—as well.

Chapter 18:
Happy People Have A Morning Ritual

For many of us, mornings begin in a rushed panic. We allow our alarm clocks to buzz at least a dozen times before deciding we have to get out of bed. Then we rush around our homes half-awake, trying to get ready for our day. In a hurry, we stub our toe on the bedpost, forget to put on deodorant, and don't pack a lunch because we simply don't have time. It's no wonder that so many folks despise the thought of being awake before 9 a.m.!

So it may not surprise you to know that the happiest and healthiest people tend to enjoy their mornings. They appear to thrive on waking up with the sun and look forward to a new day of possibilities. These people have humble morning rituals that increase their sense of well-being and give their day purpose.

Here are 3 morning habits that healthy and happy people tend to share:

1. **They wake up with a sense of gratitude**

Practicing gratitude is associated with a sense of overall happiness and a better mood—so it makes sense that the happiest and healthiest people we know start the day with a gratitude practice. This means that they're truly appreciative of their life and all of its little treasures. They practice small acts of gratitude in the morning by expressing thankfulness to their partner each morning before they rise from bed. They may also write about their gratefulness for five minutes each morning in a journal that they keep by their bedside.

2. They begin every morning anew

The happiest and healthiest people know that every day is a brand-new day—a chance to start over and do something different. Yesterday may have been a complete failure for them, but today is a new day for success and adventure. Individuals who aren't ruined by one bad day are resilient creatures. Resiliency is a telltale sign of having purpose and happiness.

3. They take part in affirmation, meditation, or prayer

Many of the happiest folks alive are spiritual. Affirmations are a way of reminding ourselves of all that we have going for us, and they allow us to engrain in our minds the kind of person we wish to be. Meditation helps keep our mind focused, calms our nerves, and supports inner peace. If you're already spiritual, prayer is a great way to connect and give thanks for whatever higher power you believe in.

Chapter 19:
5 Ways Quitting Something Can Bring You Joy

Do you ever wonder if you will ever be truly happy in your life? Do you wonder if happiness is just a hoax and success is an illusion? Do you feel like they don't exist? I know a friend who felt like this a little while ago. At the time, she was making a six-figure income, was working for her dream company (Apple), and had a flexible work schedule. Despite all this, she was miserable. She would have never been able to quit my job if not for the practice she got from quitting little things.

Of all the things that she tried, quitting these seven little things made her the happiest.

1. Quit Reading the News

News headlines are usually about happenings around the world. Most times, they are negative. Negative headlines make for better stories than positive headlines. Would you read a headline that says 'Electric Chair Makes a Comeback' or a headline that says 'Legislation debate in Tennessee'? See what I mean.

Journalists have to write stories that interest us. I can't blame them for that. Changing the time that I caught up on the news helped me be more positive during the day. Start reading inspirational posts first thing in the morning instead of news. You can still catch the news later, around 11 am instead of at 6 am.

2. Quit Hunching Your Shoulders

This boosted my confidence levels.

We hunch our shoulders and take up as little space as possible when we feel nervous and not too comfortable. This is body language 101.

Keeping a posture, opening up your shoulders will make you feel more confident during the day. But, I must admit it will make you more tired than usual. It will take you at least a total of 45 days before you start doing this effortlessly.

3. Quit Keeping a Corporate Face at Work

We are all trained not to show real feelings at work. Having a corporate face is good for corporate, not for you. Smiling all day, even when you are upset, will lift your mood. It will make you feel better sooner. Studies have shown that smiling makes you happy.

4. Quit Writing Huge Goals

It is better to write and work towards achievable goals before starting to write our stretch goals. Stretch goals are great to push ourselves. But, we all need achievable goals to boost confidence and to have successes that we can build momentum on. This can be hard for you if you are an overachiever.

5. Quit Eating Fries and Eat Oranges Instead

Fries are comfort food for a lot of people. But eating them saps energy.

Eat oranges instead of fries every time you feel down and feel the need for comfort food. This not only boosts your energy but will also help you lose some pounds if you want to. Plus, this will give you energy and clarity of mind.

Chapter 20:
10 Habits of Kamala Harris

Kamala Harris smashed the world's record by being the first Black-Asian Woman Vice President of the United States and has held high-level roles early in her career. Her career kicked off as a lawyer and quickly rose to prominence for high-profile handling cases. Her efforts could later land her the position of the district attorney, which elevated her to new heights when she was elected as California Attorney General, and US Senator.

With her empathetic, communicative, and leadership style, Kamala Harris exudes an executive presence that makes her an outstanding leader. Moreover, seeing her in a high position, addressing the nation, conveys that women can achieve everything they set their minds to.

Here are 10 Kamala Harris habits that are worth mentioning.

1. Gender Isn't a Limit.

Kamala is an inspiration to women's success in male-dominated fields. Gender, according to her, should not limit you from pursuing your dreams just because they are stereotypically not for you. She believes that both men and women should have equal access to resources for achieving greatness.

2. Make Informed Decisions

The choices you make today will have a significant impact on your future. According to Harris, tackle everything with due diligence. Having served in the public service for many years, she understands the importance of making informed choices or decisions.

3. Family Comes First

Some Professions demand huge sacrifices, which is why you should have your family closer for a shoulder to lean on. Kamala believes that if it were not for her family's help, she would not have excelled both as a lawyer and a politician. Remember that while others might leave your side during challenging times, your loved ones will never.

4. Don't Sit Around and Complain, Do Something!

Let's face it, it's either you choose to take action or continue complaining about things and not bother. During the Wilmington protest, Kamala thanked her mother for these wise words; "don't sit around and complain, do something." Every day she allows her mother's sentiments to inspire her daily tasks, which is why she is always winning.

5. Nothing can be more delightful than a smart joke.

Kamala's knack for humor helped her in winning hearts. Remember how she reacted to Donald Trump Jr.'s tweet mocking her laugh? The former president mocked her laugh and jokes as long and lame. Her response was just delightful, "You wouldn't know a joke if one raised you."

6. Her Executive Presence

Communicating as a leader is much more than what you say; it also includes your ability to dominate a room and make your presence known. Assessing how Harris makes a speech or speaks during an interview reveals that she effortlessly communicates with authority and elegance. She is not hesitant to allow her personality and femininity to shine through. Her vibrant personality, general friendliness, and captivating grin make her appear very approachable and trustworthy.

7. Connect Ambition With Purpose

As she stated in her memoir "The Truths We Hold: An American Journey," Harris's only goal was to be the solution, which saw her participating in bill formulation and change activism throughout her career. Although she got ridiculed following her rose to prominence, Harris is an example of why you should clarify your ambitions to drive you through your purpose.

8. Have a Voice To Stand for Your Values

There is no doubt that the US can feel Kamala's striking voice. She has been both an active writer and public speaker, even criticizing Trump's administration's failure to handle COVID-19 accordingly. She told the "New York Times" that when you're in a room with everyone expecting you to use your voice with pride and in a way that represents them, you realize how powerful your voice can be.

9. Flaunt Your Achievements

Harris introduced herself during the "Virtual Democratic National Convention" via her prosecutorial stories to familiarize herself with voters, highlighting her accomplishments in fighting gang and gang-related violence, sexual assault, and other issues. Women have been humbled as a result of patriarchy's consequences in order not to offend others. Like Harris, a little hot air is required to rise to get the job or any other role.

10. Show Your Vulnerability

As a leader, expressing vulnerability shows that you are also human. It also shows that you can relate to those listening to you. Harris does not shy off –of who she is and the challenges she faces.

Conclusion

Like Harris has demonstrated, be a leader that speaks up, chooses changes, stands your ground, and always acts with grace.

Chapter 21:
10 Stress Management Tips

Most students experience significant amounts of stress, and this stress can take a significant toll on health, happiness, and grades. For example, a study found that teens report stress levels similar to that of adults. Stress can affect health-related behaviors like sleep patterns, diet, and exercise as well, taking a larger toll. Given that nearly half of the survey respondents reported completing three hours of homework per night in addition to their full day of school work and extracurriculars, this is understandable.

1. Get Enough Sleep

Students, with their packed schedules, are notorious for missing sleep. Unfortunately, operating in a sleep-deprived state puts you at a distinct disadvantage. You're less productive, you may find it more difficult to learn, and you may even be a hazard behind the wheel. Don't neglect your sleep schedule. Aim to get at least 8 hours a night and take power naps when you need them.

2. Practice Visualization

Using guided imagery to reduce stress is easy and effective. Visualizations can help you calm down, detach from what's stressing you, and turn off your body's stress response. You can also use visualizations to prepare for presentations and score higher on tests by vividly seeing yourself performing just as you'd like to.

3. Exercise Regularly

One of the healthiest ways to blow off steam is to get regular exercise. Students can work exercise into their schedules by doing yoga in the morning, walking or biking to campus, or reviewing for tests with a friend while walking on a treadmill at the gym. Starting now and keeping a regular exercise practice throughout your lifetime can help you live longer and enjoy your life more.

4. Take Calming Breaths

When your body is experiencing a stress response, you're often not thinking as clearly as you could be. A quick way to calm down is to practice breathing exercises. These can be done virtually anywhere to relieve stress in minutes, and are especially effective for reducing anxiety before or even during tests, as well as during other times when stress feels overwhelming.

5. Practice Progressive Muscle Relaxation (PMR)

Another great stress reliever that can be used during tests, before bed, or at other times when stress has you physically wound up is progressive muscle relaxation (PMR). This technique involves tensing and relaxing all muscles until the body is completely relaxed.

With practice, you can learn to release stress from your body in seconds. This can be particularly helpful for students because it can be adapted to help relaxation efforts before sleep for deeper sleep, something students can always use, or even to relax and reverse test-induced panic before or during a test.

6. Listen to Music

A convenient stress reliever that has also shown many cognitive benefits, music can help you to relieve stress and either calm yourself down or stimulate your mind as your situation warrants. Students can harness the benefits of music by playing classical music while studying, playing upbeat music to "wake up" mentally, or relaxing with the help of their favorite slow melodies.

7. Get Organized

Clutter can cause stress, decrease productivity, and even cost you money. Many students live in a cluttered place, and this can have negative effects on grades. One way to reduce the amount of stress that you experience is to keep a minimalist, soothing study area that's free of distractions and clutter.

This can help lower stress levels, save time in finding lost items, and keep roommate relationships more positive. It can also help students gain a positive feeling about their study area, which helps with test prep and encourages more studying. It's worth the effort.

8. Eat a Healthy Diet

You may not realize it, but your diet can either boost your brainpower or sap you of mental energy. A healthy diet can function as both a stress management technique and a study aid. Improving your diet can keep you from experiencing diet-related mood swings, light-headedness, and more.

9. Try Self-Hypnosis

Students often find themselves "getting very sleepy" (like when they pull all-nighters), but—all kidding aside—self-hypnosis can be an effective stress management tool and a powerful productivity tool as well.

With it, you can help yourself release tension from your body and stress from your mind, and plant the seeds of success in your subconscious mind with the power of autosuggestion.

10. Use Positive Thinking and Affirmations

Did you know that optimists actually experience better circumstances, in part, because their way of thinking helps to *create* better circumstances in their lives? It's true! The habit of optimism and positive thinking can bring better health, baetter relationships, and, yes, better grades.

Learn how to train your brain for more positive self-talk and a brighter future with affirmations and other tools for optimism. You can also learn the limitations to affirmations and the caveats of positive thinking so you aren't working against yourself.

Chapter 22:
Dealing With Stress from All Angles

Stress is something that every human being suffers at some point in their lives. Whether it is A bad day at school or an exam gone wrong, there is no limit to the reasons behind stress. But some people deal with stress which does not only have one reason. In today's day and age, the world has become so fast that people do not have time for themselves. In situations where one gets the feeling of being beaten or lost, one should never give up and should always focus on what is good.

As stated by Dr. Helen Odessky, "I would encourage [you to] try A stress relief activity three times before you give up on it. "She further explains that when A person is undergoing A state of stress, the body resists any relaxation exercise or practice, so trying it out A few times increases the chances of that practice to work. Sometimes, A person's routine can make them stressed, for example, and if somebody wakes up just before the office starts, they would have to rush for the office and is likely to skip breakfast. If this is A trigger for the stress to kick in, stress can be overcome by simply changing the morning routine and giving the body enough time to function properly before the office starts.

The most important thing to notice in A stressful person is that they either breathe too quickly or too slowly because, in A time of stress, breathing is one aspect that often gets ignored. Breathing is the key for the body to function properly, so trying out A simple inhale/exhale exercise in A time of stress can help to overcome it quickly. Another thing one does in A time of stress is that they start to overthink, and the majority of the thought are negative ones. So, according to bizzie gold, who is A personal development and wellness expert, writing down your thoughts in A time of stress is A good way of letting them out. Especially the bad ones. This way, your brain would be at ease, and you can always reflect on these thoughts once the stressful period is over. Physical exercise is another good way to overcome stress as it produces endorphins, which instantly lighten the mood. The repetitive physical movements can help to fend off the bad thoughts and reset the mind, which leads to A stress-free state of mind. Even during A busy day, going for A short workout such as running can help ease the mind. Lastly, A very effective yet ignored way of overcoming stress is cleaning up the space around you. A dirty or messy space can also lead to bad thoughts, so opting for A quick tidy-up is A very good practice for overcoming stress.

Stress is indeed A very harmful feeling which can make the affected person do harmful things like drugs or alcohol, which can further lead to A messed up life. So overcoming stress before it gets A hold of you is always the better option. The exercises explained above may seem very simple but are very effective for people who deal with stress. Being grateful for what you already have is A great way to overcome stress. Find people who make you feel good in your time of need. We only have one life; why not enjoy it fully and not waste it stressing over meaningless stuff.

Chapter 23:
How Not To Control Everything

Steve Maraboli once said, "You must learn to let go. Release the stress. You were never in control anyway." Now, it goes without saying that things flow much more smoothly when you give up control when you let them be natural when you allow them to happen instead of making them happen. Being a control freak can drain so much of your mental energy without you even knowing it. It can cause you to fall into a never-ending loop of overthinking. We obsess over controlling every aspect of life without realizing the negative effects it can cause to our health, goals, and relationships. We grab them so tightly until we suffocate and kill them eventually.

Mastering the art of letting go and not controlling everything is not easy, but we should trust our instincts and know that it will be okay no matter the circumstances. We should always open ourselves to opportunities and possibilities. The path that we control and attach ourselves desperately to isn't always the right one. There would be other valuable and productive paths if we naturally and smoothly sail onto them. Letting go of control means more freedom, peace, joy, support, and connection.

It will be hard at first, but once you get your hands on it, it'll become easier and easier for you.

The first and foremost thing to do is to use your imagination. We often find ourselves overthinking the worst possibilities that could happen to us. It's like using all of your energy, time and head on climbing the steepest mountain when you can take the stairs easily and free yourself from all the stress. So, the next time you find yourself in a controlling mindset, think of all the emotional and physical energy that you might drain in trying to control a simple situation. Embrace the freedom of not having to climb that mountain and just let go and wait for whatever it is that's going to happen.

Control is usually rooted in fear. But, understand that fear is merely an illusion, its false evidence may appear real, but it's very much fake. We control things because we fear what might happen if we don't. We attach ourselves to expectations and then set ourselves up for disappointment. So, focus on grounding yourself. Take a walk in the park, meditate, relax your mind. The positive energy will only flow in when the negative energy flows out.

Have a firm belief in yourself and practice saying affirmations. Deduct any self doubts that you have and keep reassuring yourself. Recognize the importance of freedom and see what it means to you. Once you start enjoying your space, the act of controlling everything will begin to annoy you.

Change your views about life. Could you work with your life, not against it? The sooner you realize that life is beautiful and on your side, the easier it will be for you not to control everything. You would be open to opportunities and would accept whatever it will give you. If life is moving you in one direction, instead of wasting your energy in resisting and fighting it, embrace it and work towards its betterment. Some things are beyond our control; only control what you can and let go of what you cannot.

Chapter 24:
How To Be A Good Public Speaker

Public speaking is perhaps the most common and greatest fear one can endure. People would instead choose to interact with snakes or clowns than people. Just hearing about the words "public speaking" can make our palms go sweaty. But there are a hundred ways to tackle this anxiety and deliver a good speech.

Everyone undergoes physiological reactions like pounding hearts and trembling hands whenever they think about speaking publicly. Be careful to avoid associating these feelings with the sense that you might make a fool out of yourself or perform poorly. On the contrary, some nerves are good. The sweating that you get from the adrenaline rush makes you more alert, and you're then ready to give your best performance. There's no guarantee that your anxiety will completely vanish when you go to the stage facing hundreds of people, but there are ways to overcome it a little. The best way is to prepare yourself beforehand. Take your time to go over your notes. Practice a lot. Audio record or videotape yourself to see where you are lacking, get an honest friend or critique who will point out your mistakes. And once you've become comfortable with yourself, be confident and go out there!

Knowing what type of audience you're going to deal with is essential. Your audience is your main ally. Knowing and understanding them should be your priority. Engage with them by grabbing their attention. Keep the focus on them. Stay flexible and gauge their reactions. Avoid delivering a canned speech because it will only confuse or lose the attention of even the most devoted listeners.

Good communication is never flawless, and trust me; nobody even expects you to be perfect. Putting in the requisite time to prepare will help you overcome your shaky nerves and deliver a better speech. Maintain eye contact with your audience and keep the focus on yourself and your message. Keep a brief outline with you, and it can serve to jog your memory and keep you on task.

Keep thinking positively throughout your speech. It will make you feel more confident about yourself. Don't give a heads up to your fear, and it'll start a cycle of negative self-talk and self-sabotaging thoughts such as "i will start to stutter while addressing them" or "i might forget these points in nervousness." These thoughts will only lower your confidence and increase the chances of you not achieving what you're truly capable of. Affirmations and visualizations are two significant steps of improving your self-confidence. Visualize being successful in your upcoming speeches and imagine the feeling of getting done with it and leaving a positive impact on others.

Prepare yourself for any interruptions, too, and analyze how well you handle them, like sneezing in the middle of your speaking or being unprepared for a question. Do you feel surprised, hesitant, or annoyed? If you cannot handle these situations better, try to self-analyze yourself and practice managing interruptions smoothly. The next time you will get even better at dealing with stuff like that.

The more you'll get confident in public speaking, the more you will avail yourself of opportunities for success. The more you push yourself to speak in front of others, the better you will become at this. Remember, it's not a piece of cake to indulge in public speaking; the more you'll practice, the more you will excel at it. And even if it takes longer, don't doubt your ability and potential, and always be confident and believe in yourself.

Chapter 25:
10 Habits of Selena Gomez

Selena Gomez is one of the sweetest celebrities you'll ever meet, and at just 29 years old, she never ceases to amaze. She has amassed a large following on all platforms with her outstanding talent, personality, and wholesome beauty! Selena is an American songwriter, singer, actress, executive producer, cooking show host, founder, and owner of the 'Rare Beauty.'

Her albums always chart at the top of the US charts, and most of all, she's won several awards, including World Guinness Records and many more. Selena has had her share of struggles from being diagnosed with Lupus, to going through a very public breakup, but has remained stronger than ever.

Here are 10 habits of Selena Gomez you can steal from.

1. Love Yourself

Selena Gomez believes in putting herself first above anything else. In an interview with NPR's Lulu Garcia-Navarro, she discussed her body image issues. She admitted being overweight and body-shamed, her kidney transplant being ridiculed, and her very public breakup with Justin Bieber. As she says, "don't allow yourself to sink; instead, believe in yourself, in your inner capabilities, and don't allow the hate to overwhelm you."

2. She Goes to Therapy

Sometimes you'll have to talk it all out to be a completely ready self-aware person. Selena, whose beauty business 'Rare Beauty donates a portion of its proceeds to promoting mental health access, spoke to Vogue Australia about how her therapy treatment molded her into the person she is now.

3. Kill Them With Kindness

Treat your haters with kindness, as battling anger with range is futile. Selena Gomez has dwelt with trolls and bullies, both online and in person-from being called out for her weight to being criticized for Lupus, kidney transplant, and some calling her out as a "weak vocalist." She continually tries not to be bothered by it and teaches her fans to be kind. "Your falsehoods are bullets, your voice is a gun, and no war in rage was ever won," she sings in a song from her Revival album. This suggests that your words have power and may impact people's lives positively or negatively.

4. Take a Break if Need Be

Being a major voice in the entertainment industry is not for the faint-hearted; take a break when necessary. Gomez understands the value of taking breaks, which allows her to reconnect with herself, her body, and her priorities. And when you have millions of followers, any setback can affect your entire existence for eternity.

5. Keep Strong

For Selena, remaining strong is ideally the way to approach life to avoid taking advantage of her. To stay strong, you'll have to maintain mental and physical positivism. And to achieve this, do things that keep you motivated and happy, no matter how tiny or big they are.

6. Starts the Day With a Positive Attitude

If your first thought when the alarm clock goes off is degrading or harsh, you're setting the tone for a negative attitude for the rest of the day. Gomez explained on Instagram live that to stay positive; she read a book called Jesus Calling every morning.

7. Girl Power

Selena Gomez has maintained close friendships with other women in the industry, including her best friend, Taylor Swift. In 2016, their friendship was frequently referred to as "squad goals." The support they portrayed to each other. You'll gain when you keep closing those who make you happy and suffer in the hands of those with pessimistic or narrow mindset.

8. Heartbreak keeps happening

Selena, like anybody else, has experienced the gut-wrenching agony of being hurt. It's not easy, and it's certainly not entertaining for anyone.

Selena is here to let you that such experiences are perfect learning opportunities. After all, everything happens for a reason.

9. Give Back

Giving back not only brings you joy but also helps you develop a stronger sense of self. Selena is designated a UNICEF Ambassador, but she has also traveled the world to make a difference in places such as Ghana, Kenya, and Nepal. She has also collaborated with WE Day.

10. Humility

Selena is a good example of "if down-to-earth" as a person. Her humility is always genuine and persistent. You don't always have to depict yourself as fancy and showy for people to like you in life.

Conclusion

If you need to make a bold step in your life, career, or any other aspect of your life, feel inspired by Selena Gomez's actions or habits. Because standing up for yourself will almost probably motivate someone else to take the courageous action required.

Chapter 26:
6 Non-violent Communication Examples For Couples

If you would like to build strong and healthy romantic relationships, Nonviolent Communication (NVC) is a brilliant place to start.. Also known as Compassionate Communication, NVC is a way to communicate with respect and empathy. It helps us to understand and meet everybody's deepest needs. It is not about 'winning,' blaming, or changing the other person. This article will give you some examples of Non-Violent Communication for couples, so you can create unbreakable intimacy and resolve conflict in a way that makes your relationship even stronger.

1. Observing Instead Of Evaluating

'Observing' means that you simply state what you see, instead of judging or evaluating it. It involves thinking dialectically. Or in other words, thinking from a more flexible or neutral perspective.

Example 1:

'***You're always late!***' would be an evaluation.

Instead, you could try saying: '***We agreed to leave the house at 9 am, but it's 9.30 am now.***'

Stating facts instead of making sweeping generalizations can prevent you from making unfair statements. Your partner will be less likely to feel defensive, so you can have a constructive conversation instead of an argument.

Example 2:

By observing, we try to avoid making assumptions.

'***You're not listening to me!***', would be an assumption (and an evaluation!)

An observation would be, '***I can see that you are texting on your phone while I am speaking to you.***'

2. Stating Your Feelings

Once you've made your observation, you can state your feelings. Here are three examples based on the examples discussed above.

Example 1:

'We agreed to leave the house at 9 am, but it's 9.30 am now. **I feel anxious.**'

Example 2:

'*I can see that you are texting on your phone while I am speaking to you.* **I feel overlooked.**'

Example 3:

'*I can see that your arms are crossed, and you are clenching your jaw.* **I feel threatened.**'

Notice that stating the feelings started with 'I feel..' and not 'You are…'

The difference is subtle but powerful. The following statements would be blaming/criticizing rather than stating feelings:

- You make me feel anxious
- You're overlooking me
- You are frightening me

By taking the 'you' out of it, your partner will find it much easier to hear what you have to say without going into defensive mode.

3. Expressing Your Needs

After observing what you see and stating your feeling, it's time to express your need. Be careful, though.

What we think we need is often just a strategy we use to get what we really need.

For example:

You don't need your partner to do the washing up every day. You might need to feel like you're in a fair and equal partnership.

You don't need your partner to come with you on a walk. You might need to feel a sense of companionship.

So, find the need within your need. You might be surprised by the solutions you uncover!

Here some examples to help you understand how to express your needs:

Example 1:

'We agreed to leave the house at 9 am, but it's 9.30 am now. I feel anxious. It's important to me to support my sister. so I want to arrive in time to help out.'

Example 2:

'I can see that you are texting on your phone while I am speaking to you. I feel overlooked, and I need to share my experience with someone.'

4. Making A Request

Finally, it's time to make a request.

(Remember, it's a request, not a demand!)

It can be helpful to use the phrase: **'Would you be willing to…'**. Try to avoid words like **'should,'** **'must,'** or **'ought to.'**

Example 1:

'We agreed to leave the house at 9 am, but it's 9.30 am now. I feel anxious. It's important to me to support my sister, so I want to arrive in time to help out. **Would you be willing to finish weeding the garden later on so we can leave as soon as possible?**'

Example 2:

'I can see that you are texting on your phone while I am speaking to you. I feel overlooked, and I need to share this with someone. **Would you be willing to put your phone away for the next 10 minutes and hear what I have to say?**'

Example 3:

'I can see that your arms are crossed, and you are clenching your jaw. I feel threatened, and I need to feel safe. **Would you be willing to continue this conversation at a different time when we are both feeling calmer?**'

It takes practice to communicate like this, and it will probably feel quite weird at first. That's totally normal! With time, you will find it more accessible, and you might be pleasantly surprised how much stronger your relationship gets.

Chapter 27:
Happy People Use Their Character Strengths

One of the most popular exercises in the science of positive psychology (some argue it is the single most popular exercise) is referred to as "use your signature strengths in new ways." But what does this exercise mean? How do you make the most of it to benefit yourself and others?

On the surface, the exercise is self-explanatory:

a. Select one of your highest strengths – one of your **character strengths** that is core to who you are, is easy for you to use, and gives you energy;
b. Consider a new way to express the strength each day;
c. Express the strength in a new way each day for at least 1 week.

Studies repeatedly show that this exercise is connected with long-term benefits (e.g., 6 months) such as higher levels of happiness and lower levels of depression.

PUT THE EXERCISE INTO PRACTICE

In practice, however, people sometimes find it surprisingly challenging to come up with new ways to use one of their signature strengths. This is because we are very accustomed to using our strengths. We frequently use our strengths mindlessly without much awareness. For example, have you paid much attention to your use of self-regulation as you brush your teeth? Your level of prudence or kindness while driving? Your humility while at a team meeting?

For some strengths, it is easy to come up with examples. Want to apply **curiosity** in a new way? Below is a sample mapping of what you might do. Keep it simple. Make it complex. It's up to you!

- On Monday, take a new route home from work and explore your environment as you drive.
- On Tuesday, ask one of your co-workers a question you have not previously asked them.
- On Wednesday, try a new food for lunch – something that piques your curiosity to taste.
- On Thursday, call a family member and explore their feelings about a recent positive experience they had.
- On Friday, take the stairs instead of the elevator and explore the environment as you do.
- On Saturday, as you do one household chore (e.g., washing the dishes, vacuuming), pay attention to 3 novel features of the activity while you do it. Example: Notice the whirring sound of the vacuum, the accumulation of dust swirling around in the

container, the warmth of the water as you wash the dishes, the sensation of the weight of a single plate or cup, and so on.
- On Sunday, ask yourself 2 questions you want to explore about yourself – reflect or journal your immediate responses.
- Next Monday….keep going!

WIDENING THE SCOPE

In some instances, you might feel challenged to come up with examples. Let me help. After you choose one of your signature strengths, consider the following 10 areas to help jolt new ideas within you and stretch your approach to the strength.

How might I express the character strength…

- At work
- In my closest relationship
- While I engage in a hobby
- When with my friends
- When with my parents or children
- When I am alone at home
- When I am on a team
- As the leader of a project or group
- While I am driving
- While I am eating

Chapter 28:

8 Ways to Create A More Positive Mindset

Are you a glass-half-empty or half-full sort of person? Studies have demonstrated that both can impact your physical and mental health and that being a positive thinker is the better of the two.

A recent study followed 70,000 women from 2004 to 2012 and found that optimistic women had a significantly lower risk of dying from several major causes of death. Positive thinking isn't magic, and it will not suddenly make all your problems disappear; rather, what it will do is make those problems seem more manageable and help you approach these hardships productively and positively. We are going to list some things that will help you develop a positive mindset.

1. **Focus On The Good Things**

Challenging situations and obstacles are a part of life, but when you face such situations, you can focus on good things, whether they are small or big. When you try to look for it, you will find the silver lining, even if it is not immediately obvious. For example, if someone cancels plans, focus on how it frees up time for you to catch up on a TV show or other activity you enjoy.

2. Practice Gratitude

Practicing gratitude has been shown to reduce stress, improve self-esteem, and foster resilience even in very difficult times. Think of people, moments, or things that bring you some kind of comfort or happiness, and try to express your gratitude at least once a day. This can be thanking a co-worker for helping with a project, a loved one for washing the dishes, or your dog for the unconditional love they give you.

3. Keep A Gratitude Journal

Studies have found that writing down the things you're grateful for can improve your optimism and sense of well-being. You can do this by writing in a gratitude journal every day or jotting down a list of things you're grateful for on days you're having a hard time.

4. Open Yourself Up To Humor

Studies have found that laughter lowers stress, anxiety, and depression. It also improves coping skills, mood, and self-esteem.

Be open to humor in all situations, especially the difficult ones, and permit yourself to laugh. It instantly lightens the mood and makes things seem a little less difficult. Even if you're not feeling it, pretending or forcing yourself to laugh can improve your mood and lower stress.

5. Spend Time With Positive People

Negativity and positivity are contagious. Consider the people with whom you're spending time. Have you noticed how someone in a bad mood can bring down almost everyone in a room? A positive person has the opposite effect on others.

Being around positive people has been shown to improve self-esteem and increase your chances of reaching goals. Surround yourself with people who will lift you and help you see the bright side.

6. Practice Positive Self-Talk

We tend to be the hardest on ourselves and be our own worst critics. Over time, this can cause you to form a negative opinion of yourself that can be hard to shake. To stop this, you'll need to be mindful of the voice in your head and respond with positive messages, also known as positive self-talk.

Research shows that even a small shift in the way you talk to yourself can influence your ability to regulate your feelings, thoughts, and behavior under stress.

Here's an example of positive self-talk: Instead of thinking, "I really messed that up," try "I'll try it again a different way."

7. Identify your areas of negativity.

Take a good look at the different areas of your life and identify the ones in which you tend to be the most negative. Not sure? Ask a trusted friend or colleague. Chances are, they'll be able to offer some insight. A co-worker might notice that you tend to be negative at work. Your spouse may notice that you get especially negative while driving—tackle one area at a time.

I have found that writing down the things you're grateful for can improve your optimism and sense of well-being. You can do this by writing in a gratitude journal every day or jotting down a list of things you're grateful for on days you're having a hard time.

8. Start every day on a positive note.

Create a ritual in which you start off each day with something uplifting and positive. Here are a few ideas:

- Tell yourself that it's going to be a great day or any other positive affirmation.
- Listen to a happy and positive song or playlist.

- Share some positivity by giving a compliment or doing something nice for someone.

Chapter 29:
How to Value Being Alone

Some people are naturally happy alone. But for others, being solo is a challenge. If you fall into the latter group, there are ways to become more comfortable with being alone (yes, even if you're a hardcore extrovert).

Regardless of how you feel about being alone, building a good relationship with yourself is a worthy investment. After all, you *do* spend quite a bit of time with yourself, so you might as well learn to enjoy it.

Being alone isn't the same as being lonely.

Before getting into the different ways to find happiness in being alone, it's important to untangle these two concepts: being alone and being lonely. While there's some overlap between them, they're completely different concepts. Maybe you're a person who basks in solitude. You're not antisocial, friendless, or loveless. You're just quite content with alone time. You look forward to it. That's simply being alone, not being lonely.

On the other hand, maybe you're surrounded by family and friends but not relating beyond a surface level, which has you feeling empty and disconnected. Or maybe being alone just leaves you sad and longing for company. That's loneliness.

Short-term tips to get you started

These tips are aimed at helping you get the ball rolling. They might not transform your life overnight, but they can help you get more comfortable with being alone.

Some of them may be exactly what you needed to hear. Others may not make sense to you. Use them as stepping-stones. Add to them and shape them along the way to suit your lifestyle and personality.

1. **Avoid comparing yourself to others.**

This is easier said than done, but try to avoid comparing your social life to anyone else's. It's not the number of friends you have or the frequency of your social outings that matters. It's what works for you.

Remember, you have no way of knowing if someone with many friends and a stuffed social calendar is happy.

2. Take a step back from social media.

Social media isn't inherently bad or problematic, but if scrolling through your feeds makes you feel left out and stresses, take a few steps back. That feed doesn't tell the whole story. Not by a long shot.

You have no idea if those people are truly happy or just giving the impression that they are. Either way, it's no reflection on you. So, take a <u>deep breath</u> and put it in perspective.

Perform a test run and ban yourself from social media for 48 hours. If that makes a difference, try giving yourself a daily limit of 10 to 15 minutes and stick to it.

Don't be afraid to ask for help.

Sometimes, all the self-care, exercise, and gratitude lists in the world aren't enough to shake feelings of sadness or loneliness.

Consider reaching out to a therapist if:

- You're overly <u>stressed</u> and finding it difficult to cope.
- You have <u>symptoms of anxiety</u>.
- You have <u>symptoms of depression</u>.

You don't have to wait for a crisis point to get into therapy. Simply wanting to get better and spending time alone is a perfectly good reason to make an appointment.

Chapter 30: 8 Steps To Develop Beliefs That Will Drive you To Success

'Success' is a broad term. There is no universal definition of success, it varies from person to person considering their overall circumstances. We can all more or less agree that confidence plays a key role in it, and confidence comes from belief.

Even our most minute decisions and choices in life are a result of believing in some specific outcome that we have not observed yet.

However, merely believing in an ultimate success will not bring fortune knocking at your door. But, it certainly can get you started—take tiny steps that might lead you towards your goal. Now, since we agree that having faith can move you towards success, let's look at some ways to rewire your brain into adopting productive beliefs.

Here are 8 Steps to Develop Beliefs That Will Drive You To Success:

1. Come Up With A Goal

Before you start, you need to decide what you want to achieve first. Keep in mind that you don't have to come up with something very specific right away because your expectations and decisions might change over time. Just outline a crude sense of what 'Achievement' and 'Success' mean to you in the present moment.

Begin here. Begin now. Work towards getting there.

2. Put Your Imagination Into Top Gear

"Logic will take you from A to B. Imagination will take you everywhere", said Albert Einstein.

Imagination is really important in any scenario whatsoever. It is what makes us humans different from animals. It is what gives us a reason to move forward—it gives us hope. And from that hope, we develop the will to do things we have never done before.

After going through the first step of determining your goal, you must now imagine yourself being successful in the near future. You have to literally picture yourself in the future, enjoying your essence of fulfilment as vividly as you can. This way, your ultimate success will appear a lot closer and realistic.

3. **Write Notes To Yourself**

Writing down your thoughts on paper is an effective way to get those thoughts stuck in your head for a long time. This is why children are encouraged to write down what is written in the books instead of memorizing them just by reading. You have to write short, simple, motivating notes to yourself that will encourage you to take actions towards your success. It doesn't matter whether you write in a notebook, or on your phone or wherever—just write it. On top of that, occasionally read what you've written and thus, you will remain charged with motivation at all times.

4. **Make Reading A Habit**

There are countless books written by successful people just so that they can share the struggle and experience behind their greatest achievements. In such an abundance of manuscripts, you may easily find books that portray narratives similar to your life and circumstances. Get reading and expand your knowledge. You'll get never-thought-before ideas that will guide you through your path to success. Reading such books will tremendously strengthen your faith in yourself, and in your success. Read what other successful people believed in—what drove them. You might even find newer beliefs to hold on to. No wonder why books are called 'Man's best friend'.

5. Talk To People Who Motivates You

Before taking this step, you have to be very careful about who you talk to. Basically, you have to speak out your goals and ambitions in life to someone who will be extremely supportive of you. Just talk to them about what you want, share your beliefs and they will motivate you from time to time towards success. They will act as powerful reminders. Being social beings, no human can ever reject the gist of motivation coming from another human being—especially when that is someone whom you can rely on comfortably. Humans have been the sole supporter of each other since eternity.

6. Make A Mantra

Self-affirming one-liners like 'I can do it', 'Nothing can stop me', 'Success is mine' etc. will establish a sense of firm confidence in your subconscious mind. Experts have been speculative about the power of our subconscious mind for long. The extent of what it can do is still beyond our grasp. But nonetheless, reciting subtle mantras isn't a difficult task. Do it a couple of times every day and it will remain in your mind for ages, without you giving any conscious thought to it. Such subconscious affirmations may light you up in the right moment and show you the path to success when you least expect it.

7. Reward Yourself From Time To Time

Sometimes, your goals might be too far-fetched and as a result, you'll find it harder to believe in something so improbable right now. In a situation like this, what you can do is make short term objectives that ultimately lead to your main goal and for each of those objectives achieved, treat yourself with a reward of any sort—absolutely anything that pleases you. This way, your far cry success will become more apparent to you in the present time. Instant rewards like these will also keep you motivated and make you long for more. This will drive you to believe that you are getting there, you are getting closer and closer to success.

8. Having Faith In Yourself

Your faith is in your hands alone. How strongly you believe in what you deserve will motivate you. It will steer the way for self-confidence to fulfill your inner self. You may be extremely good at something but due to the lack of faith in your own capabilities, you never attempted it—how will you ever know that you were good at that? Your faith in yourself and your destined success will materialize before you through these rewards that you reserve for yourself. You absolutely deserve this!

Final Thoughts

That self-confidence and belief and yourself, in your capabilities and strengths will make you work towards your goal. Keep in mind that whatever you believe in is what you live for. At the end of the day, each of us believed in something that made us thrive, made us work and move forward. Some believed in the military, some believed in maths, some believed in thievery—everyone had a belief which gave them a purpose—the purpose of materializing their belief in this world. How strongly you hold onto your belief will decide how successful you will become.

Chapter 31:
10 Habits of Adele

There's no denying it, Adele Laurie Blue Adkins, better known as Adele is a musical legend. She is an English singer-songwriter and all-time great vocalist with excellent lyrical and passionate composing skills. Adele is one of the world's best-selling music artist, having sold over 120 million records worldwide.

With her exceptional voice and songwriting skills, the singer from a rough side of the town has captivated the hearts of millions of people. Adele got her admiration as an award-winning music legend, but moreover, there is much more from a lady who has overcome adversity to reach the top.

Here are 10 habits of Adele that will serve your learning journey.

1. **It's Far From Easy**

Criticism came thick and quick after Adele signed her first record deal because of her physical appearance. Many people, including Record label executives and high-profile designers publicly chastised her as "too fat" while suggesting weight loss to attract a larger fan base. Adele didn't let such criticism weigh in her talent as she unapologetically made hits after hits. Just like Adele, don't try to be anything or anyone but yourself.

2. **Commitment Is Success**

Despite constant pressure from the media to conform to their ludicrous notions of what women in the spotlight should look like, Adele chose her path and remained committed to being herself. This honesty is one of the attributes that Adele's fans admire. Such personality traits will breed your success.

3. **It's Okay To Be Sad After a Breakup**

When a relationship ends, you believe in acting tough and putting on a solid face. You're convinced on being tough to appear as you're suffering less than your ex-partners to win in some way. Adele defies expectations by telling her exes and the rest of the world about her grief without fear. She exemplifies humanity and vulnerability through her music.

4. **Don't Take Life Too Seriously**

It's okay to laugh at yourself or a hilarious scenario from time to time. Whether she's being teased in an interview or asked whether she wants to be a Bond Girl, Adele always respond with "Hahaha". She is quick to laugh, and her laugh is contagious.

5. Adversity Doesn't Stop Anything

Allow your pain to drive your mission. What if Adele waited till everything was back to normal before recording? All in all, people rushed to get her music, which she recorded in her misery. Every minute, every day, life happens and so should you commit to completing your projects without unconditionally.

6. Mirror Your Brand To Reflect Longevity

Say it quietly: Adele's tracks would have hit ten, twenty, or even fifty years ago. To call them timeless is a bit of a stretch. The fact may be that they're essentially personal because we believe that her music is basically from her life or personal experiences. However, Adele is always true to herself and then she sings authentically which is a formidable brand blend.

7. There Are Other Better Places Than the Spotlight

Adele doesn't constantly boost her social media presence and create "news" for constant consumption. Instead, she vanishes to do bizarre things like live and breathe and then reappears when she has something she hopes people would appreciate. It's tempting to feel the need to keep fulfilling it, but according to Adele, being true to yourself is more fulfilling.

8. Build Your Team, Not Just Yourself

When a technical issue nearly derailed her performance at Grammy Awards, Adele didn't cast an evil eye at her sound engineer. Not only did she make herself appear good by ending her performance properly, she also made her entire team look excellent. The question is, what do you do when life tosses you a curveball that you can't control?

9. Keep Going

Even when things are out of your control, it's easy to quit when everything seems to go wrong. But your perseverance will be rewarded!

10. Remember Where You Came From

Don't let your past or upbringing hold you back from achieving your goals in the future. Success is defined not by what you have as a child but by your level of commitment and work ethic over time. However, once you get there, don't forget where you come from.

Conclusion

You are characterized not by your physical appearance but by how you treat people and the words you use while communicating with everyone. Hence, just like Adele, have the confidence to pursue your aspirations. You never know where the road may take you.

Chapter 32:

Conflict Is Not Abuse

Relationship conflict can be a significant source of stress. When the conflict in your relationship is ongoing, it creates stress that can negatively affect the health and well-being of both you and your partner. Here are a few ways that conflicts in a relationship can affect you physically and mentally, as well as some tips for how to cope. Relationship conflict is a disagreement between people (e.g., partners, friends, siblings, or co-workers). The root of the conflict might be something like a difference of opinion, experience, taste, perspective, personality, or beliefs.

Conflict is generally intense enough to disrupt some aspect of the relationship, such as communication, which is what differentiates it from simply having a different point of view. It's not just romantic partners who can experience relationship conflict—families can also be in conflict. Whether it's open debate over dinner or an underlying feeling of discomfort that remains unspoken, family conflict can cause a significant amount of stress. It might be that there's no lack of love between members, but rather, a lack of comfort in dealing with conflict.

While it can be difficult and uncomfortable, conflict in a relationship is not always a bad thing. When it is healthy and productive, relationship conflict presents an opportunity for people to learn about how others see and experience the world. It can also generate creative solutions to problems and help people grow. However, when conflict is not productive or healthy, it can be harmful to everyone involved. Sustained, unresolved conflict can create tension at home or at work, can erode the strength and satisfaction of relationships, and can even make people feel physically sick or in pain.

Research has shown that relationship conflict can negatively affect your health. For example, researchers at Portland State University's Institute on Aging studied more than 650 adults over a two-year period. The researchers found that "stable negative social exchanges" (in other words, repetitive or prolonged conflict) were significantly associated with lower self-rated health, greater functional limitations, and a higher number of health conditions. These findings impact several health factors, but one key takeaway seems to be that stress can weaken your immune system.

Exposure to conflict can make you more susceptible to infectious illnesses like colds and the flu. Some people also experience chronic pain related to stress, such as headaches and back or neck pain. Those country songs about the pain of a broken heart might actually be backed up by science. Takotsubo cardiomyopathy (also known as stress cardiomyopathy or "broken heart syndrome") is triggered by extreme and sudden emotional trauma or physical stress.

"Broken heart syndrome" typically causes severe pressure-like chest pain, similar to what someone would feel when having a heart attack. Research on social exclusion has revealed that the pain of loneliness and social rejection is processed by the same area of the brain that processes physical pain, which is why it can physically hurt to be rejected by a loved one.

Conflict between partners or within families can also lead to the condition. When you are repeatedly exposed to stress and conflict in a relationship, you might develop a heightened sensitivity to physical pain or even become numb to it. Relationship conflict is not the same as abuse. If your partner is physically or emotionally abusive—whether in the presence of a conflict or not.

Chapter 33:
6 Ways To Be More Confident In Bed

Confidence is something a lot of people inherit naturally, while others could work on. When you're confident and comfortable in your skin, people assume that you have a reason to be, and then they react and respect you accordingly. You can be confident all you want at work or on dates, but what about being confident in bed? Being confident sexually can be enjoyable for both you and your partner. It isn't just at ease sexual, but also it's comfortable with the way you express and experience your sexuality.

Sexual confidence can be measured by how authentically you can relate intimately either with yourself or your partner and how pure and vulnerable you are in that sexual space where you feel like giving your 100 percent to be yourself and communicate the pleasure you desire.

Building your confidence in bed can crucially improve your sex life. Here are some tips on how to be more confident in bed.

1. Do What You're Already Confident In

Even if you are insecure and think you lack sexual skills, there must be at least a tiny thing that you might be good at. Maybe you don't feel confident enough about your kissing skills, but you're a great cuddler, or perhaps you feel shaky about touching and teasing but are good vocally. Focus on what you're good at and polish that skill every time you're in bed with your partner. This will help you boost your confidence and might even convince you to try something new with them.

2. Try Something New

Once you start considering yourself as the master of that one skill you have been practicing, you would end up craving to try new things. Start with the things you're less comfortable with; maybe stepping out of your comfort zone might be enjoyable for you after all. You neither have to perfect the skill nor be a master of it, just trying it out can be fun in itself. It might be helpful to broaden the sexual script so that it doesn't look the same every time and bore your partner, but instead, trying new things can be an excellent adventure for you as well as your partner.

3. Laugh It Off If You Trip Up

You can't be good at everything you try in bed, nor should you be. What matters is how well you keep your attitude, and if you can have fun with it and have a great laugh if things go south, that's an achievement in itself. If you have already built up consistent self-confidence, then you can laugh it out loud on something that you can't get a grip on. After all, there might always be some things you'll be bad at and others in which you'll be a master.

4. Focus On What You Love About Your Body

There are instances where we will be utterly insecure about our bodies and features. There are some physical traits that we don't like but have made peace with, while others that we want but don't appreciate enough. The next time you look in the mirror, focus more on what you like about your face and body, be confident in them, and the things you don't like about yourself will vanish automatically.

5. Wear What Makes You Feel Confident

There is no particular stuff you have to wear or the way you have to look to feel more confident, but if you wear a look that you think looks great, you must go with it. Chances are, you will start feeling better about yourself instantly. If you feel more confident wearing lipstick, then wear it to bed, or if you think sexier wearing a lotion, use it before bed. Do whatever makes you feel like a total hottie.

6. Repeat A Mantra

We have all heard of the phrase "fake it till you make it." So, there's no harm in faking affirmations till you start believing in them. Keep repeating "I'm confident, I've got this" till it gets through. Affirmations increase how positively we feel about ourselves.

Conclusion

The task of becoming confident may seem daunting, but these small sub-tasks are an easy way to start. Another plus point is once you have practiced these techniques in bed, the confidence will spill over into every area of your life.

Chapter 34:
Happy People Celebrate Other People's Success

What a phony smile... Why do people want him? How has he accomplished anything? It's ME they need. I'm the one who should be successful, not him. What a joke." This was my inner dialogue when I heard about other people's success. Like a prima donna, I seethed with jealousy and couldn't stand to hear about people doing better than me. But all the hating got me nowhere. So I thought about who I was really mad at...it wasn't the successful people I raged at. When I got more serious about succeeding, I channeled that useless envy into accepting myself.

I practiced self-acceptance with a journal, through affirmations, and by encouraging myself—especially when I failed. Then something weird happened. I started feeling happy for other people's success. Without a hint of irony, I congratulated people on their hard work, and I applauded their success with my best wishes. It felt good. I felt more successful doing it.

> **"Embrace your uniqueness. Time is much too short to be living someone else's life." – Kobi Yamada**

My writing career caught fire at the same time. I was published on sites that I'd only dreamt of, and whose authors I had cussed for doing things that the egotistical me still hadn't. Congratulating others started a positive feedback loop. The more I accepted myself, the more I celebrated other people's success and the more I celebrated their success, the more success I achieved. Now that I look back, I could've hacked my growth curve by celebrating others' success as a daily ritual.

1. It conditions you for your own success

Feeling good for someone else's success helps you generate the same feelings you need for your own accomplishments. So put yourself in the other's shoes. Revel in their accomplishments; think of all the hard work that went into it. Celebrate their success and know that soon you'll experience the same thing for yourself. Apply the good feelings to your visions for a brighter future.

2. You'll transcend yourself

Everyone knows that to actually succeed, you need to be part of something bigger. But most people are kept from that bigger something by wanting all the focus for themselves. it's an ego issue.

Through celebrating others, you'll practice the selflessness it takes to let go of your tiny shell and leap into the ocean of success that comes through serving others. Cheer your fellow entrepreneurs. Feel their success. Let go of your want for recognition and accept that you'll get it when you help enough other people.

Chapter 35:
10 Habits of Serena Williams

Serena Williams is one of the greatest tennis players of all time. To win 23 grand slams, she had to overcome obstacles that most tennis players don't face: she is a black woman in a predominantly white sport, grew up in a poor neighbourhood that was not always safe, she endured intense scrutiny of her body, racism, and misogyny.

Despite this, she still manages to be an exceptional tennis player. Williams has epitomized the grit, resilience, and mental toughness required to overcome every obstacle and hardship she has had to endure since the beginning of her career, hence inspiring athletes worldwide.

Here are 10 habits of Serena Williams for your life lessons.

1. Make Your Path

Your path is unique to you and only you. Serena has never followed a script. She was raised in Compton, California, trained by her father, mostly eschewed the junior circuit-the traditional path to tennis success.

Her emergence on the scene as a teenager player to embracing her physical prowess and chiselled figure says it all. She told Robin Roberts in an interview that she is only up to win, and inspire people.

2. Adapt Well

To maintain success, you must welcome change. Adaptability includes the ability to recover rapidly from adversity. Serena Williams demonstrates her adaptability by playing on the scorching hot hard court of the Australian Open, the slick clay of the rainy French Open, and the quick grass of Wimbledon. That implies that she delves deep when necessary.

3. Enjoy the Moment

When it comes to stressful situations, Serena enjoy seizing the opportunity to differentiate herself from the competition. Does she ever doubt herself? Yes! She accepts it, bottle it up, and toss the bottle away. Her mind-set is one that you can grasps.

4. Fuel a Work-Life Balance

Bring your entire being to everything you do. Serena's work-life balance is well-documented: she is a minority owner of the Miami Dolphins, makes her clothing and footwear, heads charity, and is a wife and mother. These outlets shape who she is as a person, and maintaining a healthy balance translates into complete focus and performance.

5. Fight Till the End

Serena has made it a point never to give up. She fights till the end in everything she does, and it has led to her incredible success. Nothing seems to break her! Coming from a poor upbringing, she has fought her way to the top. You may not be able to move or serve as she does, but you can always fight as she does.

6. Focus

Williams once stated, "if you can keep playing tennis when someone is shooting a gun down the street, that's focus!" Thanks to the tough times in her Compton upbringing, Serena has been focusing her way up to success.

7. Have Faith

Serena Williams' self-assurance over the tennis courts has allowed her to dominate. Her physique is not that of a "typical thin tennis player," but she accepts herself regardless while inspiring and encouraging other women. Having faith in every possible way in your life keeps you dominating and moving.

8. Shake It off Sooner

After qualifying for the Australian Open in 1998, Serena didn't have the best opening match, as she lost the first set. But she was not going down without a struggle. Her outstanding comebacks since then are well renowned. It's not over yet, just be present! You're still in it, and you'll have to battle for it.

9. Don't Give a Damn What Others Think

Williams has faced a lot of sexism and racism, mainly because of her physical appearance, which has been a significant factor in her domination. She has always been vocal on such criticism as well as encouraging women facing similar scepticism to heed not to what is said. As an aspiring female athlete, you can't afford the terror of being defined as "having too many muscles" and being mocked or labelled unattractive bring you down.

10. Believing in Oneself Can Be a Lonely Endeavour

People always doubted Serena's return after child delivery. But she always stated on several occasions that ignoring the odds and what others think is a critical component of overcoming hurdles and ultimately reaching success. When no one else believes in you, you have to believe in yourself.

Conclusion

Just like Serena Williams, no matter what your life's circumstances are, as an aspiring athlete or whatever your situation, keep your focus intact. Stay strong and always find a way of being a winner.

Chapter 36:
8 Ways To Love Yourself First

"Your task is not to seek for love, but merely to seek and find all the barriers within yourself that you have built against it." - Rumi.

Most of us are so busy waiting for someone to come into our lives and love us that we have forgotten about the one person we need to love the most – ourselves. Most psychologists agree that being loved and being able to love is crucial to our happiness. As quoted by Sigmund Freud, "love and work … work and love. That's all there is." It is the mere relationship of us with ourselves that sets the foundation for all other relationships and reveals if we will have a healthy relationship or a toxic one.

Here are some tips on loving yourself first before searching for any kind of love in your life.

1. Know That Self-Love Is Beautiful

Don't ever consider self-love as being narcissistic or selfish, and these are two completely different things. Self-love is rather having positive regard for our wellbeing and happiness. When we adopt self-love, we see higher levels of self-esteem within ourselves, are less critical and harsh with ourselves while making mistakes, and can celebrate our positive qualities and accept all our negative ones.

2. Always be kind to yourself:

We are humans, and humans are tended to get subjected to hurts, shortcomings, and emotional pain. Even if our family, friends, or even our partners may berate us about our inadequacies, we must learn to accept ourselves with all our imperfections and flaws. We look for acceptance from others and be harsh on ourselves if they tend to be cruel or heartless with us. We should always focus on our many positive qualities, strengths, and abilities, and admirable traits; rather than harsh judgments, comparisons, and self-hatred get to us. Always be gentle with yourself.

3. Be the love you feel within yourself:

You may experience both self-love and self-hatred over time. But it would be best if you always tried to focus on self-love more. Try loving yourself and having positive affirmations. Do a love-kindness meditation or spiritual practices to nourish your soul, and it will help you feel love and compassion toward yourself. Try to be in that place of love throughout your day and infuse this love with whatever interaction you have with others.

4. Give yourself a break:

We don't constantly live in a good phase. No one is perfect, including ourselves. It's okay to not be at the top of your game every day, or be happy all the time, or love yourself always, or live without pain. Excuse your bad days and embrace all your imperfections and mistakes. Accept your negative emotions but don't let them overwhelm you. Don't set high standards for yourself, both emotionally and mentally. Don't judge yourself for whatever you feel, and always embrace your emotions wholeheartedly.

5. **Embrace yourself:**

Are you content to sit all alone because the feelings of anxiety, fear, guilt, or judgment will overwhelm you? Then you have to practice being comfortable in your skin. Go within and seek solace in yourself, practice moments of alone time and observe how you treat yourself. Allow yourself to be mindful of your beliefs, feelings, and thoughts, and embrace solitude. The process of loving yourself starts with understanding your true nature.

6. **Be grateful:**

Rhonda Bryne, the author of The Magic, advises, "When you are grateful for the things you have, no matter how small they may be, you will see those things instantly increase." Look around you and see all the things that you are blessed to have. Practice gratitude daily and be thankful for all the things, no matter how good or bad they are. You will immediately start loving yourself once you realize how much you have to be grateful for.

7. Be helpful to those around you:

You open the door for divine love the moment you decide to be kind and compassionate toward others. "I slept and dreamt that life was a joy. I awoke and saw that life was service. I acted, and behold, and service was a joy." - Rabindranath Tagore. The love and positive vibes that you wish upon others and send out to others will always find a way back to you. Your soul tends to rejoice when you are kind, considerate, and compassionate. You have achieved the highest form of self-love when you decide to serve others. By helping others, you will realize that you don't need someone else to feel complete; you are complete. It will help you feel more love and fulfillment in your life.

8. Do things you enjoy doing:

If you find yourself stuck in a monotonous loop, try to get some time out for yourself and do the things that you love. There must be a lot of hobbies and passions that you might have put a brake on. Dust them off and start doing them again. Whether it's playing any sport, learning a new skill, reading a new book, writing in on your journal, or simply cooking or baking for yourself, start doing it again. We shouldn't compromise on the things that make us feel alive. Doing the things we enjoy always makes us feel better about ourselves and boost our confidence.

Conclusion:

Loving yourself is nothing short of a challenge. It is crucial for your emotional health and ability to reach your best potential. But the good news is, we all have it within us to believe in ourselves and live the best life we possibly can. Find what you are passionate about, appreciate yourself, and be grateful for what's in your life. Accept yourself as it is.

www.ingramcontent.com/pod-product-compliance
Lightning Source LLC
Chambersburg PA
CBHW072203100526
44589CB00015B/2343